The Project Has Landed...

by
Nicky Smith

www.nickysmith.me

This book is dedicated to my ever suffering wife Lian without who's encouragement in the form of constant nagging that "look" all women seem to be able to do from birth and all micky taking aside loving support I wouldn't have come this far...

Introduction

This whole writing thing has kind of taken me by complete surprise I knew I enjoyed doing it to summarize mostly to myself what I had done on my first ever Land Rover rebuild but when I started to post it on different Land Rover forums and the members started to both follow comment share and encourage my ramblings I was astounded that other people wanted to read my drivel as well as follow what I was up to but the proof was really in the pudding of it all folk seemed to like what I was doing.

Armed with this little bit of encouragement I typed away each time I did anything to my old Series 3 FFR Land Rover and folk carried on reading it so much so I have decided to put it all in one place along with the feedback comments that I received some good and some just downright taking the mickey out of my ineptness!

But why did I decide to rebuild a Land Rover in the first place? Well I had hit the big 40 stopped smoking decided to get a bit fitter than I had been in a long time (having hit the halfway point in life longegevity had become an attractive proposition) and I wanted to see something that would have been my Ciggerette money. I wanted to show myself that I was doing the right thing trying to live long enough to embarress the grandkids. Landy's had always appealed so I started saving the money up and soon enough a project I could afford came along and the rest as they say is history.

Anyways thats enough rambling from me please jump in enjoy the book I am the user id min200 and feel free to leave any feedback you feel appropriate...everyone else did.

The Project Has Landed...

min200

The project has landed!

Went and had a look at an ex military series 3 on Monday and after having a good nose around and under I bought it!

The chassis looks like new but the rest of it needs some work...not too much but enough to make a good project :)

I managed to get delivery included all for the princely sum of £375 :D:D

To say I'm chuffed is an understatement!!!

Here's a few pics.

yellow90

Re: The project has landed!

nice project , 12v or 24v electrics?

min200

Re: The project has landed!

24 volt. Guess I best get saving for the expensive bits!

timc1967

Re: The project has landed!

Amazing price. Looks like it just needs a bucket & sponge then register for the road.

Andyzwright

The project has landed!

That looks really cool. Well done. I look forward to following your progress!

min200

Re: The project has landed!

Quote:

> Originally Posted by timc1967 (Post 3031240)
> *Amazing price. Looks like it just needs a bucket & sponge then register for the road.*

:D Yea see you all on Sunday lol where are we heading!

Scho1

Re: The project has landed!

great find!

Buz

Re: The project has landed!

Nice looking project, interesting to follow the work

generaldogsbody

Re: The project has landed!

That's gonna look great.

min200   25th-April-2014 20:53

Re: The project has landed!

Well I started the deep clean today. I figure clear all the rust and rubbish then I can see exactly what needs doing. Turns out its an ex communications vehicle and has lots and lots of extra radio wiring through out but I will be removing this.

Only got about an hour in on it before the heavens opened but hopefully get some time in this weekend :)

Huddy84   26th-April-2014 00:30

Re: The project has landed!

Looks good. Another one rescued from delapidation. Look forward to seeing it develop.

Re: The project has landed!

The deep clean.

I awoke today to find it raining heavily which put a stop to any early work on the Landy today so a morning of running around doing family chores it was. I hate picking up all of the bits we need as a family just call me old fashioned but dog food and choosing paint colours is just plain dull!

But the sun broke through just after lunch so I dropped whatever it was I was supposed to be doing in the house, something about cleaning drawers out comes to mind but who knows what it was Wifey had in mind, and set to the Landy with a scraper and a dust pan and brush.

It's amazing what difference a good clean out can do and what you can find!! I knew there were a couple of bits of what I thought was junk in the back of it but what I found surprised even me!
A near perfect wing to replace my dented one!
A spare wheel the rim is sound but the tyre is perished.

SO with all of that out I scraped and swept the back of the landy until it was rubbish free!
I am still surprised at how well the body on this old motor has held up. I was expecting a lot more rot!

I then started on removing some of the old military bits that were no longer needed for the radio equipment it used to haul. I did get a little carried away with myself though and soon realised I had taken two bits of the 24v system from behind the seats...I promptly called myself a knob and put those back on!

The only piece of rot I have found so far is in the passenger foot well and that's nothing major!
I also WD40'd all the leaf springs and nuts and bolts underneath that I could find. I figured this is worth doing a few times as the old girl has been stood for a couple of years!

That's all today but we shall see what tomorrow will bring.

owl   26th-April-2014 22:41

Re: The project has landed!

I converted a few 24 volt motors to 12 volt many years ago and we used to get a good price for all the 24 volt stuff we took off, It might be worth trying not to damage it and putting it up for sale.

min200   27th-April-2014 07:45

Re: The project has landed!

I was thinking of just leaving it at 24v. What would need to be changed to convert it to 12v? I have read so many conflicting theories!

Kwakerman   27th-April-2014 09:23

Re: The project has landed!

I would hazard a guess at:
All bulbs and relays,
Starter motor
Alternator
Wiper Motor
Heater motor
Coil

Fuel / Temp gauges (unless they are on a 12V regulator)

min200

Re: The project has landed!

I was planning to get a couple of batteries together and test the electrical system before I strip down the landy. If everything works ok I will leave it but if its riddled with problems I will do a full strip down and start again with a 12v loom.
I want this old girl to last me years so may as well do it properly!

timc1967

Re: The project has landed!

Years ago I read that 24v is a great system and it is possible to live with it. I wonder if you Can split it to get 12v bulbs and so on but keep the starter etc?

easye1

Re: The project has landed!

nothing to do with 24 volt landies
(though your find is an absolute gem matey)
but I used to run 24volts to a 12 volts starter motor on my race
cars ;)
the 12volt feed to the starter ran through the second 12volts battery
= had 24 volts to spin the old style starter...

spun over "nicely"

min200

Re: The project has landed!

Scraping paint
Main
Posted by min200 Sun, April 27, 2014 17:29:33

Just a small potter today. I don't know why but I feel out of sorts like
something isn't quite right but I cant put my finger on it? Either a
bug coming on I expect as the kids have been coughing and
sneezing for a few days (don't you just love those little plumbers!) or
it's just my body and mind winding down from a couple of weeks in
the transport office arguing with drivers who want their arses wiped
for them.

Anyways after he days chores were done I didn't feel like doing a lot
but the weather is good and the landy is on the drive so I thought a

paint scrape was in order to remove the layers and layers of loose paint off of it. The army are good at paint jobs, if it needs a new colour you just thickly paint over the old one! Cant fault them its cheap and effective but its going to take more than a paint scraper to get it back to a decent even level so I have ordered some sanding discs to help the job on.

After that was done I decided to have a quick stab at removing the old antenna mountings off of the sides and was pleasantly surprised when they came off nice and easily!
Not a massive difference but these little steps add up!

Had an hour on Ebay as well looking at parts for it and have ordered sanding discs, new ignition barrel and a letter from Heritage stating the year of its build etc.

Landy Project Costs

Land Rover £375

Sanding Discs £11.70

Ignition Barrel £20

Heritage letter £21.75

TOTAL £428.45

min200

Re: The project has landed!

Quote:

> Originally Posted by easye1 (Post 3035072)
> *nothing to do with 24 volt landies*
> *(though your find is an absolute gem matey)*
> *but I used to run 24volts to a 12 volts starter motor on my race cars ;)*
> *the 12volt feed to the starter ran through the second 12volts battery = had 24 volts to spin the old style starter...*
>
> *spun over "nicely"*

Thanks folks I'm pleased with it so far! A stab at the 24v circuit first I think then take it from there ;)

easye1

Re: The project has landed!

Quote:

Landy Project Costs

Land Rover £375

Sanding Discs £11.70

Ignition Barrel £20

Heritage letter £21.75

TOTAL £428.45

---

nice....
never been one to stop a man from working, but, have you tried a good jet washing of the flaky paint areas to see just what you can move with intense water jets.

min200

Re: The project has landed!

That was my original plan. I took the jet wash out of the shed plumbed it all up ready to go and nothing! Turned out the motor has seized over the winter :(Im not running out to buy a cheap one as the old Karcher has given me years of service so I will save up and buy a decent one again.

The Landy would have needed sanding anyway as there must be 6 layers of paint on it...probably one of the reasons its lasted so well :laugh:

easye1

Re: The project has landed!

The Landy would have needed sanding anyway as there must be 6 layers of paint on it...probably one of the reasons its lasted so well ....
lol..
dont knock it eh....paint does cover all metals/alloys very well if enough is applied..

min200

Re: The project has landed!

Oiling up.
Main
Posted by min200 Tue, April 29, 2014 11:30:21

Nothing much happening on the project as we are into the working week. I did get time to have a look around the engine bay and WD40 up any moving parts that needed it along with the spark plugs seeing as they look pretty well rusted in place.
I had another good look around the bulk head and apart from the one bit in the passenger footwell it really is solid! It amazes me that something can last out so well when its just been dumped in the corner of a yard for years!

There are also twin fuel tanks under the seats which I hadn't noticed before so im learning as I go with this one.

Nothing else new ordered for it....yet.

Re: The project has landed!

The letter from the Heritage Motor Centre arrived today with the Landy's date of birth.

It was made at the Lode Lane factory, Solihull on the 8th August 1983. This letter will help with registering it with the DVLA once the rebuild is done and the motor has an MOT.

Of course I have been spending more money and today picked up a couple of batteries and a rear quarter light. These were needed because the replacement ignition has arrived so it will be good to see what electrics if any work on it!

The only bits I have done today to the Landy are starting to disconnect the wiring toi the nearside wing which will be removed later this week.

I have Wednesday and Thursday off this week so I'm hoping to make some serious headway on the welding.

Landy Project Costs

Land Rover £375

Sanding Discs £11.70

Ignition Barrel £20

Heritage letter £21.75

2x Batteries and rear 1/4 light £35

TOTAL £463.45

easye1

3rd-May-2014 15:00

Re: The project has landed!

love it matey....

must admit its a shame your jet wash is not working, as looking under that bonnet its crying out for a good spring clean, and being 24 volt would assume its pretty watertight ....
maybe one of my fetishes, a good jet wash....lol..just love clean things......
was even parked in tescos car park waiting for the mrs today - and I just had to look under my bonnet to see how clean it all is after yesterdays engine bay jet wash...:)

Landtom

3rd-May-2014 18:29

Re: The project has landed!

Bit of chassis cleaner all over it and a power wash and it'll be as good as new! Great wagon great price does it run? What engine has it got?

min200

Re: The project has landed!

A pressure washer would be nice but its broken :(BUT.....I will be getting aother soon enough if I get my way ;)
You had best check the engine bay again in the morning just to be sure its still clean, its a long way back from Tescos.

It's a 2.25 petrol and it turns free enough but as for running watch this space :)

min200

8th-May-2014 14:34

Re: The project has landed!

I've been looking forward to a couple of days off so I could get stuck into the Land Rover again but the weather hasn't been on my side. I did get to do a fair bit yesterday before the heavens opened for good but today it has been raining since I got up so I shall take solace in hunting ebay for bargain parts that I need but cannot afford.

So yesterday I jumped up bright and early to the comment from Wifey of "Why don't you have a lie in?" You would think that after 15 years together she would know I ma still a big kid at heart and with something as tempting on the drive as I have sleep is an awkward chore that just has to be done in the shortest time possible!

My plan of attack was straight forward...I wanted to weld up those holes in the passenger foot well. First off was the near side wing as this is very badly dented and out of shape and the replacement is waiting in my shed to be fitted. I disconnected all of the wiring for the lights and figured out a bolt at a time exactly where abouts they were all located by thinking to myself "well that should come off now" only to find it wouldn't and then searching for the offending bolts they fitted as overkill at the factory.

Whilst taking off the wing I realised that the front bumper was in a bad state of affairs and could do with replacing so it was whipped off using a wheel brace and brute force.
With all of this of I could now access the front floor well without having to perform contortionist acts with a welder in my hand. The area was ground back to give me some clean metal to weld to and off I set with the welder...

The welder wouldn't work and it took me some time to figure out why the feed wasn't playing. It wouldn't feed because the top couple of layers of weld had gone rusty, when I thought back to the welders last use I realised it was over four years ago so it wasn't surprising really. With the rusty wire stripped out off I went to weld and play again. The floor pan is now hole free but the rain kicked in before I got to grind my over enthusiastic welds down so that's my first job for when the weather clears.

The "Artic Weather heater" that's in this Landy has bits all over the place including this heater in front of the radiator!

So I think I will strip the lot out altogether once the bodywork is sorted.

After stripping the wing off I found the normal heater to have rusty holes in it and on the bracket mounting it to the body work so this was stripped out ready for a replacement once I get to the putting it back together stage.

The only thing ordered this week are a pair of battery clamps for the terminals. Once the weather clears I will be starting on the painting of he chassis I can reach and then the refitting of the floor pan that was removed whilst I was welding.

Landy Project Costs

Land Rover £375

Sanding Discs £11.70

Ignition Barrel £20

Heritage letter £21.75

2x Batteries and rear 1/4 light £35

Pair Battery Terminal Clamps £3.99

TOTAL £467.44

elan23

Re: The project has landed!

That ain't no heater, that's an oil cooler. (We live and learn)

min200

Re: The project has landed!

Quote:

> Originally Posted by elan23 (Post 3049762)
> *That ain't no heater, that's an oil cooler. (We live and learn)*

Indeed we do! Thanks for that chap I will leave it in place then eh :pound:

DOH!!! But a good save :)

easye1

Re: The project has landed!

Quote:

> Originally Posted by min200 (Post 3043700)
> *A pressure washer would be nice but its broken :(BUT.....I will be getting aother soon enough if I get my way ;)*
> *You had best check the engine bay again in the morning just to be sure its still clean, its a long way back from Tescos.*
>
> *It's a 2.25 petrol and it turns free enough but as for running watch this space :)*

Oh, as its been pi$$/pouring with rain today,

so our beachfront road being as bumpy as feck, had big puddles to splash through....

frightened to look under the bonnet in case its got dirty :rolleyes:

but on a better note, keep the log going on your new baby...

and as you commented on being asked for a lie in by the mrs, ohhh, dont neglect the needs of the swimbo....
you`ll pay fit it later!

min200

Re: The project has landed!

I wasn't lucky enough to be invited to stay in bed with the wife and have a "lie in"...She was already up and ready for work lol

min200

Re: The project has landed!

It's Alive!
Main
Posted by min200 Fri, May 09, 2014 10:34:47

Seeing as the rain had held off this morning and I have some time to kill before work I decided to see if I could get the electrics on the old girl fired up. I wired up a new battery connector link, not bad for the total cost of less than £6, and set to replacing the ignition barrel.
In a rather unusual turn of events this all went very well with no major problems arising or bits falling off as I was doing it so all was wired up in less than 20 minutes.

Now was the moment of truth...I turned the ignition on and there was life!! The wiring loom works across the board and the engine turns over nicely, I knew the engine wasn't seized but it is nice to hear the starter motor working after being parked up in the corner of that farmyard for so long!

I even managed to find all of the screws for the steering column cover and put that back on along with freeing up the choke cable. So I am like a kid at Christmas now happy that the 24v system can stay in but seeing as that Artic heater was working just fine I am back in two minds about taking it out again! Thankfully there is plenty to do so no rush to make that decision.

Iann
9th-May-2014 14:14

Re: The project has landed!

I like it and your a jammy git at that price :D

min200
9th-May-2014 22:01

Re: The project has landed!

Quote:

Originally Posted by Iann (Post 3050930)
I like it and your a jammy git at that price :D

I have been called worse...and yes I am a total jammy git!

Re: The project has landed!

Steady Progress
Main
Posted by min200 Sat, May 17, 2014 19:34:57

I have done a few things over the last couple of days but the tinterweb was down so I couldn't update!

Started to underseal the chassis and bulkhead, I had forgotten what a messthat stuff makes and how the hell does it end up all over you even when you think you are being careful! Still the results are great with the chassis looking like new.
There is still plenty to do under there but at least two thirds is done which is nice!

I have repaired and refitted the old heater I removed as it is 24v and if I can save a few pennies here and there all the better. After refitting I tested it and it works perfectly.

Next step is going to be refitting the replacement wing along with loosening up the exhaust bolts at the manifold because whilst undersealing I noticed the exhaust has been more or less completely flattened in one stop under the chassis so will need to be replaced. Im quite glad I have seen it if I am honest because it would have been a pig of a job once the wing was back on!

min200

Re: The project has landed!

Landy Project Costs

Land Rover £375

Sanding Discs £11.70

Ignition Barrel £20

Heritage letter £21.75

2x Batteries and rear 1/4 light £35

Pair Battery Terminal Clamps £3.99

Floor pan nuts & bolts £6.50

TOTAL £473.94

min200

Re: The project has landed!

Primer
Main
Posted by min200 Mon, May 19, 2014 16:20:03

I have been taking advantage of the glorious weather we have been having which has arrived at the same time as my days off of work which has been superb!

Saying that by taking advantage of I mean I have been out and about most of the time on my motorbike but I have still managed to get a couple of bits done.
I sanded down the bodywork trying to remove some more of the layers upon layers of paint that the Army have slapped on but I don't think I will ever get a completely smooth surface, still this will ad to the character of the old girl I suppose!

I primed up some of the rusty areas under the bonnet and on the front panel.
Then I set about patching a few holes in the body work where old bolts used to come through making sure I made the two patches on the roof watertight.
My next big removal problem is inside there is an old radio rack fitted to the floor that had flat head screws through to welded bolts underneath the floor. I cant get to the bolts with a grinder and the flatheads are either seized solid or rusted enough so as to give no purchase. Maybe I will grind off the old uprights and use this old rack as some sort of holder. No rush to decide it's not in the way.

Once its a bit cooler I will finish the under sealing of the chassis then we will be onto the mechanical side of things which I am looking forward to!

min200

Re: The project has landed!

Landy Project Costs

Land Rover £375

Sanding Discs £11.70

Ignition Barrel £20

Heritage letter £21.75

2x Batteries and rear 1/4 light £35

Pair Battery Terminal Clamps £3.99

Floor pan nuts & bolts £6.50

Grinding disc £2.25

TOTAL £476.19

easye1

Re: The project has landed!

all looking good mate.

min200

Re: The project has landed!

Quote:

Originally Posted by easye1 (Post 3064079)
all looking good mate.

Thanks steady away progress wise and it always looks like you have done bugger all!

min200

25th-May-2014 19:50

Re: The project has landed!

Not a lot done to the Landy Project due to the crap weather!

I refitted the passenger side floor pan today along with new nuts and bolts. Also filled up the radiator with water to check for leaks as I have promised my nephew that we will try and get the old girl running when he visits next weekend.

Oh the Landy has also been named.....we shall call him "Mator" as in the rusty old pick up in the film Cars. Thanks to a close family friend, you know who you are, who came up with it last week and now its stuck whenever I try to talk about anything Land Rover related!

min200

28th-May-2014 11:44

Re: The project has landed!

Well I have been jumping underneath Mator the Landy between rain storms Trying to get the under sealing finished but as I was making some really good headway in a rain free couple of hours I ran out of underseal.

So a quick trip to the shops to buy some more, and my god hasn't the stuff gone up in price!, I gave the rain a chance to blow back in and it's now coming down in a steady drizzle the type of when you look out you think "It's not too bad" but within minutes you are drenched. No more playing out today before work now then.

On a more positive note I have just bought a whole new/replacement set of 24v lights for the old girl so that's another major parts find scrubbed off of my list.

I must pick some petrol up before Saturday so my nephew and I can try and start it.

Landy Project Costs

Land Rover £375

Sanding Discs £11.70

Ignition Barrel £20

Heritage letter £21.75

2x Batteries and rear 1/4 light £35

Pair Battery Terminal Clamps £3.99

Floor pan nuts & bolts £6.50

Grinding disc £2.25

Under Seal £8.99

Complete set of lights £85

TOTAL £570.18

easye1   28th-May-2014 14:52

Re: The project has landed!

lol....

me, from the old school I`m afraid, and bought so many cars for banger racing in the long ago past, that the first thing we done was to see if the bloody thing ran, normaly on the end of a rope on the way home from purchase :D
even if the motor had to come out to be fitted with a "racing" lump..

even now, I`d never be so dam patient as you in getting it running....lol

but saying that, I cant fault you methodical approach to it all.
good luck, and keep the updates coming....
great reading....

lorri789   28th-May-2014 18:59

Re: The project has landed!

Yes. Keep us posted on the work :)

min200   28th-May-2014 23:25

Re: The project has landed!

Thanks folks! The updates will keep coming ;)

Patient...me?...Nah just too tight to buy the petrol lol

min200

Re: The project has landed!

Racking & Bolts
Main
Posted by min200 Sat, May 31, 2014 19:11:06

Today the last of the FFR racking came out of the Landy along with more bolts than I can believe! Honestly I must have removed quarter of a ton in metal from the motor!
Still looks a lot better in there now with access from the front to the back without having to get out and walk around to each door!

This also involved moving the seat belt holders to the side panel. Now these seat belts are about knackered but I wanted to make sure the bolts were the right size for the holes on the side and if I am honest I am not sure the actual belt tensioners are mounted in the right place as they seem to snag at a funny angle when the belt is returned.

Then my Brother and nephew arrived so the big moment had come to see if I could get the old thing running. I put some fuel into the drivers side tank switched the changeover to RH side...

And nothing. It turned over fine but no firing up. Now I am not sure if I have the tank switch on the right tank and will endeavour to find out.
Not to be defeated I poured a little fuel into the carb and it fired up on the first turn of the key and ran for about ten seconds!!!! SO the

engine runs just fine! It will need a good service but it will be staying in for now :)

All in all a pretty good day!

RobertOHare

Re: The project has landed!

them mud flaps are mint.

easye1

Re: The project has landed!

""Not to be defeated I poured a little fuel into the carb and it fired up on the first turn of the key and ran for about ten seconds!!!! SO the engine runs just fine!""

best way mate..
at least you now know it runs --- that WAHOOOOO moment :)

min200

Re: The project has landed!

    Quote:

It was indeed! I don't know who was smiling more me or my nephew!

Iann

31st-May-2014 21:59

Re: The project has landed!

you may have to remove the pipe off the fuel pump and give it a suck (good job for the nephew) to prime it up and find out if the switch over tap works

Thats if it a mechanical pump, if its ellecy its easier

Go steady with the spending you may be getting close to half the normal buying price :D

min200

Re: The project has landed!

Quote:

Originally Posted by Iann (Post 3080158)
you may have to remove the pipe off the fuel pump and give it a suck (good job for the nephew) to prime it up and find out if the switch over tap works

Thats if it a mechanical pump, if its ellecy its easier

Go steady with the spending you may be getting close to half the normal buying price :D

I shall have a look later today if I get time. The nephew being used as a tool so I don't get fuel in my mouth??!! I have to say that that is a superb idea!

As for the costs of this little project I do realise that the spending is running away with itself and I will try to keep a check on it

min200

Re: The project has landed!

Well after grabbing 30 minutes to myself this morning I have had a good nose through the fuel system. It has a manual primer much like an old diesel? and a clear glass bulb that you could see the fuel sitting in if it was coming through at all.

But there is no fuel coming through at all and if im honest the fuel pipes look past their best as well as there being jelly in the bottom of the glass bulb. It's the old fuel that's been sat in there that long its turned bad and reduced to jelly!

So I will have to strip down the whole fuel system so I have the opportunity to change it over from twin tanks if I feel like it but at the moment I am not sure. I will be taking the drivers wing off for access to the fuel lines and pumps as well as the brake and clutch cylinders so do I go the whole hog and stick a 200tdi lump in it or do I keep it original 24v petrol...decisions decisions.

Iann

Re: The project has landed!

How about getting it all up and running and live with it for a while before you decide on and engine swop
It will be on the road quicker
and if you decide to do an engine swop you can source the parts at your leisure while running it

Andyzwright

The project has landed!

Keep it original, is that not the point of an ex army rebuild? However, I appreciate economy is important too. I think similar to the post above, get it going and see how you use it and how it works out

min200

Re: The project has landed!

You guys are probably right! I am in a mix of get it on the road asap and take my time to get it bang on right.

On the road will win though I expect!

min200

Re: The project has landed!

Scrubbing.
Main
Posted by min200 Tue, June 03, 2014 16:18:37

I had quite a lot of time on my hands today because I don't have to be at work until this evening for my last CPC course (what a bloody waste of time and an obvious money maker for those in control but that's another whine for another day)

SO as I looked first at the sky hoping the clouds would keep their water then at the dog who sat there with her lead in her mouth I went for a wander and contemplated what to do for the day. I had ordered some primer for the Landy over the weekend but it hadn't arrived yet, that was until I got home! There sat on the doorstep was my big shiny tin of primer! So my day was planned!

First I poked out the Landy's eyes that were full of water and then set to scrubbing the roof down as it still had some dirt layers and mould on from the the years it was stood.
And whilst I was throwing water around I even gave the engine bay a good scrub down!

A rumbling stomach halted play as gave time for the water to dry off but then I got stuck into sanding down the bonnet and roof. This done and a wipe down later it was time for the primer to come out!

I set to using a cheap gloss roller from Wilkinsons as I had read somewhere that it worked quite well on metal. Seeing as this old motor will never be a show course car I thought I would give it a go and I have to say it works very well!
This is just the first coat and I expect it will take at least 3 to give a reasonable finish but considering I was starting with a pigs ear paintwork wise the results so far are promising! Its also really nice to see some progress on the outside rather than just underneath!

Landy Project Costs

Land Rover £375

Sanding Discs £11.70

Ignition Barrel £20

Heritage letter £21.75

2x Batteries and rear 1/4 light £35

Pair Battery Terminal Clamps £3.99

Floor pan nuts & bolts £6.50

Grinding disc £2.25

Under Seal £8.99

Complete set of lights £85

5 Litres Primer £24.99

TOTAL £595.17

Andyzwright
3rd-June-2014 18:32

The project has landed!

Good work. Great post, keep it up (work on the Land Rover and the post!)

Chris W
3rd-June-2014 18:58

Re: The project has landed!

looking good :D

marccleave
3rd-June-2014 20:33

Re: The project has landed!

What colour will you be going for on top of the primer? The primer reminds me of a southern electric land rover almost.

timc1967

Re: The project has landed!

A transformation. It looked awful before but now i can see your vision.

easye1

Re: The project has landed!

yep, looking good mate.
I cant believe just how good its come clean under the bonnet areas....almost new looking..lol

min200

Re: The project has landed!

Quote:

> Originally Posted by marccleave (Post 3084089)
> *What colour will you be going for on top of the primer? The primer reminds me of a southern electric land rover almost.*

Thinking white roof with nato green on the rest of it at the moment but seeing as I haven't bought any paint yet I am sure that will change!!

min200

Re: The project has landed!

Quote:

> Originally Posted by timc1967 (Post 3084119)
> *A transformation. It looked awful before but now i can see your vision.*

Funnily enough the Wife said that!

min200

Re: The project has landed!

Quote:

> Originally Posted by easye1 (Post 3084172)
> *yep, looking good mate.*
> *I cant believe just how good its come clean under the bonnet areas....almost new looking..lol*

I knew you would like that picture!

easye1

Re: The project has landed!

Quote:

> Originally Posted by min200 (Post 3084752)
> *I knew you would like that picture!*

lol...with me, its whats under the bonnet comes first, the rest is what everyone else sees ;)

sorry, but its been in my blood since I can walk really....:D

min200

Re: The project has landed!

Last week was my long rota week at work so I didn't do a lot on the Landy but this week has been my short week so two uninterrupted days off mid week whilst the kids are at school and Wifey is at work so I got stuck right in!

With our annual holiday fast coming up cash is tight so I have been doing the few bits I can without spending anymore cash. So first up was scraping off the loose paint on the back end and then putting on the first coat of primer. A second coat of primer was then put on the rest of the bodywork as well as on the back end.

I havn't done the door as its scrap, well the front ones are as well but one coat of primer makes the old girl look a bit better on the drive!
I managed to get the rear lights undone as they were seized solid and then I set to attacking the old frame that held the radios to the rear floor when it was in use as a comms unit. They were flat head screws into two bolts that were seized solid so I had to attack the framework with a grinder. This was all done on the inside because I couldn't get the grinder anywhere the bolts underneath. After twenty minutes of grinding and banging and swearing the bloody thing came out!

Then I set to finishing the last of the underseal. I bloody hate that job but finally it is all done along with my arms and the clothes I was wearing. So good riddance to that job.

Now I am hunting hard for a cheap set of doors to put on then once painted the bodywork will be done.

min200

17th-June-2014 11:58

Re: The project has landed!

Had a spare hour this morning so I thought I would follow the fuel system through and see if it was a simple fix like a split pipe or seal gone somewhcre I had suspected the primer pump was knackered but it all looked ok.

This proved fruitless after climbing under in and around the Landy. When I dropped the seat base trapping my finger between it and the seat frame I had had enough. When I saw the blood I just laughed to

,myself thinking that this was the icing on the cake!

So I took a few minutes out sticking a plaster on my finger wondering what the hell could be the problem with this twin tank system. That's when I decided it may be better to have fuel in both tanks even though there is a tank switch as it is literally the only thing I hadn't done.

A quick trip to the petrol station later I put the fuel into the empty side tank and tried to prime the pump....the fuel pulled through no problem at all! At this point I started to get my hopes up and pulled the choke out gripped the key and gave it a turn....

It fired straight up and revved its nuts off so I pushed the choke in and it still revved its nuts off so off it was turned again! Talk about happy though the fuel system works!

After a bit more looking around the carb I am pretty sure the needle is stuck but if a carb rebuild is all I need to do I am very pleased! Im still looking for the ever elusive body parts but it will probably be new doors the way I am going.

The next thing to buy after the doors will be a clutch cylinder to see if that can be freed up or whether it will need replacing.

Not a bad morning at all :)

min200

Re: The project has landed!

Fuel System Part 2
Main

Posted by min200 Wed, June 18, 2014 11:48:31

After some feedback from readers of my blog I have been informed of a few things and put them into place.

The reason my engine is running its nuts off is this...
There is a hand throttle and is fitted in FFR Land Rovers and when this is pushed over to the fully on position the engine does indeed gat a bit lively!

So after putting this in the off position the engine started lovely and ticked over nicely. I let it run a while and then once the coolant had warmed up a bit I tried the artic heater and hey presto lots of lovely hot air blowing in from all directions. So this little bit of kit can stay in the rebuild :)

There isn't a needle in the carb on the landy and this was a presumption on my part after working with classic mini's for years! So with that in mind and the obvious oversight on the hand throttle I have come to the conclusion....

That I do not know what I am DOING!!!

I took off the end dash panel to check the wiper motor over and was greeted with a lovely shower of rust so another part to be replaced has been added to my list.

But still cant complain as so far I am still on the right side cost wise on this rebuild :)

generaldogsbody   18th-June-2014 14:53

Re: The project has landed!

Ye man,told you it would look good.

DiscoMatt77 18th-June-2014 21:43

Re: The project has landed!

I'm jealous, that looks great! Be interested to see what you do with it.

min200 18th-June-2014 22:33

Re: The project has landed!

Its coming on and will be used as a toy at weekends but as for the final product......watch this space ;)

DiscoMatt77 19th-June-2014 22:23

Re: The project has landed!

I'm definitely gonna watch with interest, I quite fancy getting one myself.

easye1 20th-June-2014 01:40

Re: The project has landed!

thanks min..you made I chuckle......lol

the way you explain everything, is a way of teaching us about your type of landrover.
never knew things about them, as I do now....
your not so daft as you feel/think/are (delete as appropiate) ;)

min200

20th-June-2014 12:56

Re: The project has landed!

Thanks guys I really am learning as I go along with this motor and at times I wonder what the hell I have started lol

I just write it as I think it....with a couple of omissions ;)

min200

23rd-June-2014 18:01

Re: The project has landed!

Spending Money.
Main
Posted by min200 Mon, June 23, 2014 17:27:22

I seem to have had my fair share of luck on ebay in the last week or so. I usually miss out on any real bargains but it seems it must have been my turn lately :)
I have picked up a rear door in excellent condition with lock and key for the princely sum of £21.
When I got there to collect it I was asked if I wanted a drivers side door bottom in nearly new condition with a bit f surface rust on for £20...yes please!
Then I had to go out and collect a set of discovery steel wheels I won for £10.20

The tyres on three are shot but one of them is more than good enough for a spare. Upon closer inspection one of the rims has a lot of weights on so I wont bother with that one as I know somewhere I should be able to pick up a couple more wheels later today.

So after unloading the car I set to removing the old back door from the Landy but I had to have the inner door handle off of it to put on the new door. I can report I actually managed to get something right by noticing the door retaining strap before I had taken all of the hinge bolts out and would have to had the door hanging off trying whilst trying to reach the right sized spanners!

So I soon had the old rotten door off and gone and the new door was fitted. There was a different retaining arm on this door but seeing as I had so carefully noticed the canvas one I removed the metal one. It wasn't as easy as I would have liked I had to bend up the flap at the end of the run and remove the rubber stopper it soon popped out and I just folded the end flap back down again.

The interior handle was then fitted to the new rear door and ta da I now have a door that locks and closes on the Landy! It's the only door that locks and closes on the Landy but hey its one more than I had this morning!

Im off to haggle on a few bits later so will update in due course...at this rate it will look like a Land Rover again soon!

Landy Project Costs

Land Rover £375

Sanding Discs £11.70

Ignition Barrel £20

Heritage letter £21.75

2x Batteries and rear 1/4 light £35

Pair Battery Terminal Clamps £3.99

Floor pan nuts & bolts £6.50

Grinding disc £2.25

Under Seal £8.99

Complete set of lights £85

5 Litres Primer £24.99

4 Discovery Wheels £10.20

Rear Door £21.00

Front Door £20.00

Handbrake spring £1.50

TOTAL £647.87

min200

Re: The project has landed!

Spending more!
Main
Posted by min200 Mon, June 23, 2014 21:41:41

Just a quick update more to keep tabs on money spent than anything else.

There's a chap called Gary over in Derbyshire that breaks and also rebuilds Landys and seems to have an endless supply of parts! Visiting this bloke can make a serious dent in your wallet!

So this evening I have bought and collected two more Discovery steel wheels, a replacement wing mirror, two headlamp surrounds, two headlamp frames and a pair of discovery seatbelts as the ones in my Landy are beyond repair.

All this for the sum of £60 so I cant complain! Hopefully he will have two new front doors at the weekend as well.

Landy Project Costs

Land Rover £375

Sanding Discs £11.70

Ignition Barrel £20

Heritage letter £21.75

2x Batteries and rear 1/4 light £35

Pair Battery Terminal Clamps £3.99

Floor pan nuts & bolts £6.50

Grinding disc £2.25

Under Seal £8.99

Complete set of lights £85

5 Litres Primer £24.99

4 Discovery Wheels £10.20

Rear Door £21.00

Front Door £20.00

Handbrake spring £1.50

2 Discovery wheels

Two seatbelts

Wing Mirror

2 Headlight surrounds

2 headlight frames £60

TOTAL £707.87

Re: The project has landed!

New Doors!
Main
Posted by min200 Wed, July 02, 2014 13:20:22

The weather has been with me this last few days and I have been geeky excited because I managed to buy a pair of half decent front doors at the weekend so onto the Landy they must go!

I was happy to find that the door hinges and bolts hadn't rusted away into scrap and they came off quite easily!

****At this point I must point out to anyone who hasn't removed doors before like me that it is far easier if you remove the door stay BEFORE removing the hinges. This will save you standing there like a pillock with a rusty door hanging in your hands whilst still attached to the motor wondering what the hell you are going to do now! Personally I stood the door back in its frame and popped a couple of bolts back through the hinges but this was after I stood like a prat with the neighbours and passers by looking at me with looks of barely held in laughter on their faces!***

So before taking the hinges off remove the end cover and remove the door stay but take the split pin out of the drop bolt and remove the bolt. Then the door will come off freely and unhindered saving any red faced embarrassment and looking around to see if anyone is watching you.

I then removed and refitted the door latches to the replacement doors.
So I did this for both doors and fitted the replacement ones. Then I rubbed them back a bit ready for priming and masked up the windows.
Time for another couple of coats of primer and the top coat paint was delivered whilst I was out painting so guess what tomorrows jobs going to be?
So a mornings work to make it look the same as it did before I started but at least the doors work and are rust free now!

There are some parts on the old doors and the old wing that I have kicking around including the window runners that I will need to put in these replacement doors. So a happy hour stripping bits off of junk to then stick on Ebay to raise some much needed funds for the project.
All in all not a bad days work but I am now happily sitting on the top of the hill and with each new task the Landy will start to look like a motor again from here on in!

Landy Project Costs

Land Rover £375

Sanding Discs £11.70

Ignition Barrel £20

Heritage letter £21.75

2x Batteries and rear 1/4 light £35

Pair Battery Terminal Clamps £3.99

Floor pan nuts & bolts £6.50

Grinding disc £2.25

Under Seal £8.99

Complete set of lights £85

5 Litres Primer £24.99

4 Discovery Wheels £10.20

Rear Door £21.00

Front Door £20.00

Handbrake spring £1.50

2 Discovery wheels

Two seatbelts

Wing Mirror

2 Headlight surrounds

2 headlight frames £60

2 Front Doors £60

Nato Green Paint £36

TOTAL £803.87

min200

Re: The project has landed!

Started Painting
Main
Posted by min200 Thu, July 03, 2014 13:31:22

It's starting to look like a Land Rover again!

I had an early finish at work last night so I got up early to collect some new rollers and git stuck in painting. With the strong breeze and sunshine I managed to get two coats on before wrapping it up for work.

I feel like im getting somewhere now :)

Iann

3rd-July-2014 13:45

Re: The project has landed!

Looking good mate

is that army green paint the brushable roller type
If so did you thin it out,

I under coated my roof today and have a tin of army roller/brush
pain and woz just going to slap it on :D

min200

3rd-July-2014 14:15

Re: The project has landed!

I just used a cheap gloss roller and a paintbrush from wilkinsons1
Seemed to do the trick ok and the paint is straight from the tin with
no thinning out :)

Iann

3rd-July-2014 14:22

Re: The project has landed!

Quote:

Originally Posted by min200 (Post 3126416)
*I just used a cheap gloss roller and a paintbrush from wilkinsons1
Seemed to do the trick ok and the paint is straight from the tin
with no thinning out :)*

Thats my plan aswell
I dont need a spay type finish on the old girl

min200

4th-July-2014 00:37

Re: The project has landed!

Easiest way to do it :)

min200

Re: The project has landed!

Lighting
Main
Posted by min200 Fri, July 04, 2014 12:36:24

Steady morning just putting the lights back on.
And then I painted up the headlight surrounds and air intake vent cover.
The chores of family life then called upon me to collect the middle
daughter from uni and now its time for work so best be back off to
the grind I don't want to do eh!

elan23

Re: The project has landed!

I'm in the middle of the same type of project though 12v and with a truck cab.
Just a couple of things though, although the 109 is 24v the ignition system runs on 12v so you could use civilian dizzy, leads, plugs and coil if you want. Secondly have you noticed that the doors you fitted don't have the hole for the lock barrel? I ended up waiting for some MOD doors to come onto ebay, pricey but I got lucky. Excellent thread though.

min200

Re: The project has landed!

Thanks for the voltage info its always good to know the odd trick :)

When I looked at the doors I realised they didn't have the lock barrel on them but its been sat on my drive for months like that and I can lock them from the inside and get out of the back so really it's not a problem for me. If someone wanted to steal it they would only have to throw a wet sponge at those type of door locks to get in lol

Im glad you like the thread Im enjoying keeping tabs on what I do to the old girl!

DiscoMatt77

Re: The project has landed!

Amazing what a difference just putting lights and grill back on makes! Looks excellent.

tyre man dave

Re: The project has landed!

its looking good mate.
need to do some work on mine
need to make an exhaust up

got a 3ltr capri essex v6 in, fired her up the other day
blow exhaust to bits sounds nice, but rather loud

tyre man dave

Re: The project has landed!

what size tyres you running.
may be able to help you out with rims /tyres.
got a few spares

min200

Re: The project has landed!

Pottering
Main
Posted by min200 Wed, July 09, 2014 12:23:32

You have got to love this dry weather! It's given me time to just potter with the landy and it's amazing how much you can get done when you are not trying to get anything in particular sorted out!

The drivers door needed the restraining bar refitting but it needed new holes drilling before I could fit the end cap on.

Then I refitted the air intake mesh. I am wondering whether or not to paint the screws green or just leave them silver...

Then onto the front of the roof. When I was painting it I realised that there were a few holes there where rivets had been before so the easiest way forward was to replace the missing rivets.
I took a look at my watch and time was heavily still on my side so I decided it was time to sort out the drivers side wing mirror.
Surprising what effect these little changes have on the whole motor!

Now it was onto the headlights which as it turns out are the standard military issue ones that differ from the civvy ones in just about every way! Luckily I had already bought the replacement headlamp frames and they were still attached to sealed units and headlight cones. I stripped out the military ones and set to fitting the civvy standards remembering to use the correct fittings and wiring. I also took the opportunity to fit the halogen conversion lamps that have been in the shed for a couple of months and the headlamp surrounds.

It's only starting to look like a proper Land Rover again! Still so much to do but I love the way its starting to look complete again!

Dr_evil

Re: The project has landed!

Quote:

> Originally Posted by min200 (Post 3129286)
> *Thanks for the voltage info its always good to know the odd trick :)*
>
> *When I looked at the doors I realised they didn't have the lock barrel on them but its been sat on my drive for months like that and I can lock them from the inside and get out of the back so really it's not a problem for me. If someone wanted to steal it they would only have to throw a wet sponge at those type of door locks to get in lol*
>
> *Im glad you like the thread Im enjoying keeping tabs on what I do to the old girl!*

If you want some doors with a lock on them I'm selling some off my series 3, they're just taking up space so going cheap

Dr_evil

Re: The project has landed!

Btw if you get it on the road and the weathers still good I'd suggest no door tops ;) I've been using mine without the tops and its lovely

easye1

Re: The project has landed!

Quote:

> Originally Posted by tyre man dave (Post 3130059)
> *its looking good mate.*
> *need to do some work on mine*
> *need to make an exhaust up*
>
> *got a 3ltr capri essex v6 in, fired her up the other day*
> *blow exhaust to bits sounds nice, but rather loud*

:D
memories matc..
3litre granadas at arena essex, best with me in one at full chat in 2nd...
awsome noise if you cut the pipes just before they joined....;)

easye1

Re: The project has landed!

Quote:

> Originally Posted by min200 (Post 3134569)
> *Pottering*
> *Main*
> *Posted by min200 Wed, July 09, 2014 12:23:32*
>
>
> *You have got to love this dry weather! It's given me time to just potter with the landy and it's amazing how much you can get done when you are not trying to get anything in particular sorted out!*

:D
be proud mate..
its looking really well for its age.....
I follow your posts eagerly.
thanks.

min200

Re: The project has landed!

Quote:

> Originally Posted by easye1 (Post 3135583)
> :D
> be proud mate..
> its looking really well for its age.....
> I follow your posts eagerly.
> thanks.

Thanks chap I am enjoying myself rebuilding it and I love the fact folk are getting something out of my inane rambling :rofl:

min200

Re: The project has landed!

More Green
Main
Posted by min200 Thu, July 10, 2014 12:08:41

I started the day having to look at the electrics of this bloody thing...

Seeing as the low beam lights had decided they were not going to work anymore it took priority because I use it daily as my hack for work. After a bit of trying to get my ape like hands in small places it turns out it needs a new relay so that will have to be sorted at the weekend.

Still onto the Landy because lets face it you don't want to be reading about a motorbike do you...

Today was another painting day!! Yay me!! More green paint to scrape off of my arms because I tend to get more on me than on the surface I am supposed to! The lucky areas today were the inside of the doors and in all fairness they needed it because they looked awful!
With the sun facing the right way and a good breeze it didn't take to long to put a couple of coats on both the doors and my arms.
Whilst I was throwing the paint about I thought I may as well give the inside that's not still covered in half stuck on and rotting sound proofing a couple of coats...
It does tidy it all up though! Trying to save some money I have started to soak the one rear window rubber that's covered in paint in a bucket of soapy water for a couple of days this is an old trick I picked up years ago it lifts the paint away from the rubber making it easy to remove and should save me a tenner or so because I should only need to buy one now.

The problem with this fitting in the rebuild before going to work is my shed is taking a hit and is a right bloody mess...
Well that's my excuse for being a lazy arsed git who doesn't want to tidy it up anyway.

easye1   11th-July-2014 18:33

Re: The project has landed!

a man can only do so much in any one day..
I used to think I could do more in a longer day, but it was a foolish
thought..

only realised that in later years..;)

you going at a great speed, keep it up, but leave enough free time
for other loves in your life..

min200   11th-July-2014 22:26

Re: The project has landed!

Wifey makes me do other stuff so no worries there! Im also changing
shift start times shortly so the work will slow down but as there are
holidays coming up funding will be down for a couple of months.
Still I am enjoying the way its coming on and doing the project
itself :)

min200   12th-July-2014 19:55

Re: The project has landed!

Water Tight...Well sort of.

Today I have had the pleasure of working an early shift in the office which gives me the pleasurable opportunity to greet all of the night shift drivers returning back to base. These guys are a special breed of folk that work the night shift because inflicting them on the general public during the day would be considered a cruel and criminal act to anyone they encountered in fact if I called these guys the most miserable bastards on the planet it really would be an insult to the most miserable bastards on the planet.

They are singularly the most ignorant and unpleasant folk I have ever met and quite frankly they are a waste of air but I just smile and be jolly in their company because this really seems to piss them off.

two o'clock soon came around and an eight hour day is a really short one in my world so I arrived home happy in spite of the nose to tail traffic on the ring road. Wifey was in and doing chores so I sat down to open the post that turned up at the same time I did. In amongst all of the flyers for pizzas and mobile phone contract offers was the new window seal for the back quarter I had ordered and seeing as I had cleaned up the other one I had soaking yesterday I set about fitting the rear windows to the Landy.

Thankfully I still had the window seal insert tool from my rebuilding mini days which made the task nice and straight forward along with the hot day that kept the rubber nice and pliable. I remember trying to put the seal insert in on a really cold day once, I soon gave up on that idea and waited for the days to warm!

So with those windows fitted it should make my Landy water tight again...well as watertight as any Land Rover gets...ummm ok then it will stop any puddles coming back where the windows were not fitted before.

Wifey and the girls were sat n the back garden by the time this was done so I sat with them cleaning up the old Discovery wheels I had bought getting them ready for some anti rust painting.

Right I'm off to a party So depending on the hangover status I may or may not get anything done tomorrow!

Landy Project Costs

Land Rover £375

Sanding Discs £11.70

Ignition Barrel £20

Heritage letter £21.75

2x Batteries and rear 1/4 light £35

Pair Battery Terminal Clamps £3.99

Floor pan nuts & bolts £6.50

Grinding disc £2.25

Under Seal £8.99

Complete set of lights £85

5 Litres Primer £24.99

4 Discovery Wheels £10.20

Rear Door £21.00

Front Door £20.00

Handbrake spring £1.50

2 Discovery wheels

Two seatbelts

Wing Mirror

2 Headlight surrounds

2 headlight frames £60

2 Front Doors £60

Nato Green Paint £36

Rear Window Seal and insert £9.99

TOTAL £812.86

min200

Re: The project has landed!

Rusty Wheels
Main
Posted by min200 Tue, July 15, 2014 10:53:26

Funds are running a little low this month now so I had to look for a job I could do with what I had to hand today and the options were rather limited.

In all honestly I couldn't be bothered with the idea of painting six wheels on both sides with anti rust primer so I took the dog for a walk.

After a gentle stroll around the park I got back and no other options had miraculous presented themselves so I got the paint out.

They looked like rusty crap to start but in all fairness it only took an hour to do all six as soon as they are dry I best be putting them away as Wifey wont think they are very nice as garden ornaments. I'm thinking of matt silver as the colour rather than anything shiny.

easye1

Re: The project has landed!

nice work as my 5yo grandson would say..

cream colour looks nice on series or fender wheels....(only just saying)

my disco wheels are painted each year with a cheap silver paint on the outside, and even cheaper rubbish paint on the insides....

min200

Re: The project has landed!

I did consider black bumpers and wheels which do look good but Im now set on some sort of matt silver if I can get it.

Is yours still fitted out with all the FFR gear or have you ripped it out like me?

Iann

16th-July-2014 14:50

Re: The project has landed!

The paint I did my roof with last week is not what I ordered
I wanted green like yours but in mat
The thing is ive had it 3 years now before opening :doh:

It looks ok though (good job two)

I remember there being contradiction in the names of paint colours on the sites on Flee bay

min200

16th-July-2014 15:17

Re: The project has landed!

LOL 3 years is quite some time to store paint chap! If I did that the "green" would end up being purple :D

It always without fail looks better with the second coat of paint on. If you want the link to the paint I bought I would be happy to post it or PM you it chap.

big red   16th-July-2014 16:41

Re: The project has landed!

Quote:

Originally Posted by min200 (Post 3143390)
Is yours still fitted out with all the FFR gear or have you ripped it out like me?

No the radio gear has gone. The boxes are behind the seats still, but that's all. I did having the racking, but like you I've taken it out and moved the seatbelts to brackets at the side.

Iann   17th-July-2014 13:33

Re: The project has landed!

Its not the dark mat green I wanted but it will do

min200   17th-July-2014 14:28

Re: The project has landed!

Gardening
Main
Posted by min200 Thu, July 17, 2014 14:24:59

Well the back garden got to the point where I couldn't ignore the mess anymore and the constant nagging about it was getting tiresome so first job of the day was to tidy that up.

This involved lots of sweating because its a sun trap out there and loading up the junk into the Dacia Sandero for the dump run.

It amazes me how much crap you can fit in a small car when you stack it right well that and the determination I was only going to make one trip!

Whilst tidying up I came across something that had come with my Land Rover so I put it to one side so I could finally find out what it is.
As it turns out it is a "Snow Blind" which makes sense seeing as the Landy has the Artic heater in it. Its of no use to me at all but a search on Ebay showed up nothing similar so I suppose there is either no call for these at all or they are difficult to come by. Either way I shall throw it up for sale to try and get some more funds together for the project.

So after the big tidy up and lawn mowing session I wondered what to do with the rest of my day off. As you may have noticed its bloody hot so nothing else too strenuous was ever on the cards and after a wander around the Landy I noticed I needed to refit the rear door strap. So I drilled a couple of new holes and hey presto strap fitted.

Then I decided it's too damned hot to do bugger all else and am now hiding indoors with a packet of ice poles :)

easye1

Re: The project has landed!

lol...
off subject slightly mate, but the sun Indeed has been burning here on the coast also.
Over the last few weeks (well, since last year if truths known) I`ve been working outside on my garden/ rear driveway project
(sorry dont do photos - but maybe soon)
but being as I`m now "banned" from strong sunlight, I purchased some garden gazebos, the better one being a 2.5 metre square pop up design, I move around to work under.
the other 3 metre Sq. one is fixed on the patio..
damm good Idea for working under them gazebos,
and with ALDI selling a cheap version @ 2.4 metres sq. in green & white for - £9.99 I bought that one also.....
No. 1 son has blagged that one for this weekends BUG JAM at Santa Pod ;)
(ps-dont tell landigirl)..lol..
so, agree, we all have to stop work on our projects when the SWIMBO`s are on the warpath, eh....

min200

Re: The project has landed!

LOL indeed we do! It is too bloody hot to do much of anything and I managed to make myself feel sick as a pig yesterday with the heat!

Still we shouldn't moan about the two weeks of good weather we get a year!

min200

Re: The project has landed!

I have been rather quiet of late for two reasons. The first is that I ran out of cash early last month to spend on the Landy and the second is we had to go on holiday with the kids to Spain for the pleasures of an all inclusive pool side holiday in Benidorm.

Now I know that sounds like me moaning and being ungrateful but I can think of more interesting things to do than sit beside a pool for a week trying not to get up and give other peoples obnoxious kids a good clout around the ear hole but seeing as I don't really drink now getting pissed daily isn't an option and my god it's amazing how quickly you get fed up of eating! Still I am lucky enough to be able to go away and for that I am grateful so here isn't the place to go on about my holiday...just pop over to my blog site to hear me do that lol.

So after doing all of the fun things that you have to do when you get back from a family holiday like picking up two carrier bags of dog shit because the dog sitter "Forgot", cleaning out three different sorts of other shit from the various pets dotted around the house and fuelling up the motorbike ready for work in the morning I had an hour spare so I snuck off to see the Landy. I had ordered some wire connectors so I spent some happy quiet time fitting those to the nearside indicator, side and headlights. I connected the batteries and let there be light!

The indicators only work on the offside if you hold the indicator stalk in just the right place and there are no hazard or fog lights working but at least the new headlights I fitted work!

I will plod along with the light wiring as and when I get a chance in between bigger jobs. I have just been paid so I best prioritise what to fix mechanically first so all ideas are welcome!

Landy Project Costs

Land Rover £375

Sanding Discs £11.70

Ignition Barrel £20

Heritage letter £21.75

2x Batteries and rear 1/4 light £35

Pair Battery Terminal Clamps £3.99

Floor pan nuts & bolts £6.50

Grinding disc £2.25

Under Seal £8.99

Complete set of lights £85

5 Litres Primer £24.99

4 Discovery Wheels £10.20

Rear Door £21.00

Front Door £20.00

Handbrake spring £1.50

2 Discovery wheels

Two seatbelts

Wing Mirror

2 Headlight surrounds

2 headlight frames £60

2 Front Doors £60

Nato Green Paint £36

Rear Window Seal and insert £9.99

Wiring connectors £3.00

TOTAL £815.86

tyre man dave

3rd-August-2014 18:20

Re: The project has landed!

HI MATE
the hazard warning switch may not need one.

recently checked with reguards to my 109 mot
the hazard warning lights came in after 1986
if yours is before 86 like mine.not needed for m.o.t.
have checked with land rover and m.o.t. tester

min200

Re: The project has landed!

That's good news then and one less problem before MOT! I will have a nose at it but if its a problem its not now!

Mine was built in 1983 so well within!

Thanks chap! Any ideas on the order of what to do mechanically now? I fugure handbrake first then clutch then brakes and steering.

tyre man dave

4th-August-2014 18:48

Re: The project has landed!

sound,s like a plan to me

Andyred90

5th-August-2014 16:32

Re: The project has landed!

That's a lot of progress in three months..Whats next?

Iann

Re: The project has landed!

Quote:

> Originally Posted by **Andyred90** (Post 3170486)
> *That's a lot of progress in three months..Whats next?*

Yes he's making me out to look lazy :D

boguing

Re: The project has landed!

Quote:

> Originally Posted by **tyre man dave** (Post 3168103)
> *HI MATE*
> *the hazard warning switch may not need one.*
>
> *recently checked with reguards to my 109 mot*
> *the hazard warning lights came in after 1986*
> *if yours is before 86 like mine.not needed for m.o.t.*
> *have checked with land rover and m.o.t. tester*

Local MOT man told me the same, but if there's a switch fitted, they must work. So remove the switch, or if it's like mine was, unscrew the top with the triangle on it.

min200

6th-August-2014 23:14

Re: The project has landed!

Quote:

> Originally Posted by Iann (Post 3171541)
> *Yes he's making me out to look lazy :D*

:D Slowed down a bit at the moment but I have a week off I very soon with very little to do so I should be making some more progress then!

Its decided that I shall do the handbrake next then the clutch so theres two forms of it not rolling down the drive into the dual carriageway :eek::eek:

Then it will be the steering bars, track rod ends and brake rebuild front and back...should be enough to be getting on with for now!

min200

Re: The project has landed!

Quote:

> Originally Posted by boguing (Post 3171985)
> *Local MOT man told me the same, but if there's a switch fitted, they must work. So remove the switch, or if it's like mine was, unscrew the top with the triangle on it.*

Now that really sounds like a plan!

Iann

Re: The project has landed!

It entirely up to you but I wired in Hazards an a fog light ,put in seat belts etc which mine didnt need for test
They are all safety items,

Coz you have stacks to do and dont need them for test you can do these if you like at your leisure

min200

Re: The project has landed!

Quote:

> Originally Posted by Iann (Post 3172828)
> *It entirely up to you but I wired in Hazards an a fog light ,put in seat belts etc which mine didnt need for test*
> *They are all safety items,*
>
> *Coz you have stacks to do and dont need them for test you can do these if you like at your leisure*

Everything will be fitted over time but I just want to get it Mot'd asap lol

min200

7th-August-2014 19:19

Re: The project has landed!

Hand Brake
Main
Posted by min200 Thu, August 07, 2014 19:12:31

Ended up with an extra day off of work today because I foolishly ate a pizza at lunchtime which triggered my IBS off big style. I got to work to happily find 5 spare drivers kicking their heels so I managed to bag the day off as a holiday which was great because I really didn't think I would have made it the distance between service station toilets on the motorway without shitting myself!

So I got home and had to potter about as it eases the pain. After sorting the imperial from the metric spanners out in the shed I went to the toilet again. After this horror I decided to have a nose at the hand/transmission brake on the Landy.

I didn't have the correct imperial size spanner for the adjusting nut as loads of my tools seem to have done a bunk but I found that the ring end of a 7mm spanner worked perfectly on it with no play. I sprayed on some WD40 and slowly worked the adjusting nut forwards and backwards a bit at a time adding more WD40 as needed until it freed up.
Then I started on removing the nuts holding the drum on and of one of these had been rounded off before but hey theres always a buggered nut isn't there!
Luckily I have a tool box full of odd old sockets so I grabbed a slightly undersized one 1/2 and hammered it into place.
This brought the knackered nut off nicely. At this point I realised that the next fart was going to be more than that and rushed to get out from under the landy smacking my head then running for the toilet wondering whether to clutch my stomach, my arse or my now banging head.

After some considerable time had passed I got back under the Landy and gave the drum a good whacking with a hammer to loosen the contents up a bit shift some muck and free off the brake pads.

Then I used a flat ended screwdriver inserted into the edge between the back plate and the drum to see if it would gently free off. Much to my surprise it came off easily and then I was very happy to see the brake pads and components where all in good condition!

So a quick clean up and the drum was put back on.

After a quick adjustment up the hand brake now works perfectly! The only component I have had to replace is the spring on the handbrake itself. Now what a bloody job that was as I was trying to force it up and over the place it was supposed to fit into whilst trying not to shit myself in the process.

So another job marked off of the list and only at the cost of a new nut, handbrake spring and a lump on my head...which is nice!

min200

Re: The project has landed!

More Paint.
Main
Posted by min200 Fri, August 08, 2014 11:52:56

Just picked up two tins of metallic paint from Wilkinsons. This stuff is basically the cheap version of Hammerite so all good. silver in colour it will be used for the windscreen frame and the wheels I have already primed.

I scraped the paint off of the windows on the landy so at least you can see out of them. Not enough tome to do anything else at the moment so the first dry day next week will see some more colour on the project!

Landy Project Costs

Land Rover £375

Sanding Discs £11.70

Ignition Barrel £20

Heritage letter £21.75

2x Batteries and rear 1/4 light £35

Pair Battery Terminal Clamps £3.99

Floor pan nuts & bolts £6.50

Grinding disc £2.25

Under Seal £8.99

Complete set of lights £85

5 Litres Primer £24.99

4 Discovery Wheels £10.20

Rear Door £21.00

Front Door £20.00

Handbrake spring £1.50

2 Discovery wheels

Two seatbelts

Wing Mirror

2 Headlight surrounds

2 headlight frames £60

2 Front Doors £60

Nato Green Paint £36

Rear Window Seal and insert £9.99

Wiring connectors £3.00

2 tins of silver metal paint £7.00

TOTAL £822.86

easye1

Re: The project has landed!

well you made me smile, then I learned that the handbrake drum comes off without taking the prop off....cheers...lol

nothing worse that fearing to fart because of impending outflows eh...;)

Little Butch

Re: The project has landed!

Love these kind of threads, gives me the inspiration to work on my 1987 110! :)
You've done a cracking job so far...

min200

Re: The project has landed!

LOL Im glad someone got some enjoyment out of my pain...from both ends :)

Thanks for the compliment Im enjoying doing it up BUT it looks like there will be a slow down in restoration as I have just got a shift change at work so am back to working day shift which is bloody great!

min200

Re: The project has landed!

Fundraising
Main
Posted by min200 Sun, August 10, 2014 18:26:36

I am fundraising for The Outward Bound Trust. These guys do great work with kids who live under the poverty line and try to install some new skills into them and show what you can achieve in life.

Basically its your life and you can achieve just about what you want to.

We are off for a week where there will be hiking and wild camping along with sailing and climbing. A lot of these kids have never been away before.

BUT before this turns into a bad TV begging advert which lets face it we are all numb to and sick to the back teeth of if you have enjoyed keeping up with my blog and if I have made you smile would you just give a pound or two please as I have to hit a target of £500 and this is what pays for the kids.

You can donate directly on this link (I have removed the link as it has now been closed down but please feel free to donate directly to "The utward Bound Trust")
Go on give us a quid it will take less time to do than reading all of this has!

min200

Re: The project has landed!

A Massive thank you to those folks who have donated! It makes me smile knowing that there are still more folk out there that give a damn than don't.
You people don't shout it from the roof tops just quietly help out and it restores your faith in humanity.

Enough of the sloppy nonsense if anyone else would be happy to part with a pound or two it would be much appreciated!

Now this is the last begging post I will post but I will post a thank you to anymore donations so thanks again folks it will make a difference to these kids.

Re: The project has landed!

Im Cursed
Main
Posted by min200 Wed, August 13, 2014 13:22:38

Over the last couple of days I am sure someone has been hiding in the trees opposite my house just waiting for me to start doing anything that is linked to the Land Rover and when I do he turns on the water.

Yesterday I got out the clutch master cylinder and just had time to check that it was the correct part before it started to rain.

Today I decided to get on with painting the replacement wheels. Having been caught out yesterday I had a look up into the sky and thought to myself "ok it's cloudy but doesn't look dark enough for rain". I proceeded to go and get changed into some old kit that I can get paint on without Wifey giving an earful on how I always manage to wreck my clothing and grabbed the key to my shed to get the paint out.

All good so far! So I rummaged around to find an old paint brush and after a few minutes had the brush and paint in hand just in time to hear the start of loud patters on the shed roof!

That was the end of that idea because there is no way I can paint six Land Rover wheels in my 8x6 shed.

So I came indoors and ordered some sand paper and new fuses for the old girl online instead. Hopefully a bit more luck tomorrow or maybe I can sneak out without that chap in the bushes noticing me.

Landy Project Costs

Land Rover £375

Sanding Discs £11.70

Ignition Barrel £20

Heritage letter £21.75

2x Batteries and rear 1/4 light £35

Pair Battery Terminal Clamps £3.99

Floor pan nuts & bolts £6.50

Grinding disc £2.25

Under Seal £8.99

Complete set of lights £85

5 Litres Primer £24.99

4 Discovery Wheels £10.20

Rear Door £21.00

Front Door £20.00

Handbrake spring £1.50

2 Discovery wheels

Two seatbelts

Wing Mirror

2 Headlight surrounds

2 headlight frames £60

2 Front Doors £60

Nato Green Paint £36

Rear Window Seal and insert £9.99

Wiring connectors £3.00

2 tins of silver metal paint £7.00

Fuses & Sandpaper £4.50

TOTAL £827.36

min200

Re: The project has landed!

Wheels
Main
Posted by min200 Thu, August 14, 2014 11:33:10

Remember how I was bragging a few posts ago about how I found a nice cheap Wilkinson alternative to Hammerite? Well ignore because the Wilko stuff is utter crap! It's like trying to paint water onto metal with the colour of cold tea regardless of what the colour is supposed to be on the tin.

So that was a waste of money but hey ho at least it didn't rain on me whilst I was playing with the stuff. Luckily I had a tin of silver spray kicking about and being the impatient bugger I am I decided to blow over the spare wheel I had with it before fitting it to the Landy to A) see what it looked like and B) actually get the poor old girl up on four wheels that had air in them giving me a little more room to get underneath etc.

Now that its on the Landy I don't know whether I want silver wheels at all. Maybe its because I have got used to the dirty mixed coulours of they existing wheels or maybe this wheel is just too silver. Maybe a darker matt silver would look better or maybe black? But Black might be too dark....bloody hell listen to me its only a set of wheels colour and most of the time they should be covered up in mud if I use it right!

Maybe they will grow on me and they will look a lot better with chunkier tyres on. Doesn't really matter for now as I don't have any more spray so I can take some time to think about it.

Little Butch

14th-August-2014 11:47

Re: The project has landed!

I'm with you, would look much better in a darker colour mate

boguing

Re: The project has landed!

A word of warning. If you value your sanity do not investigate shades of silver. There are more of them than colours in a rainbow. I'm still on the pills six years after doing some Alfa wheels.

Black, lime white, or matching green. Leave it there and walk away without a backward glance.

min200

Re: The project has landed!

LOL you are probably right!! Im already leaning towards black.

min200

Re: The project has landed!

Going for black wheels
Main
Posted by min200 Fri, August 15, 2014 12:13:55

After some deliberation I have decided to go with black wheels. I had to nip into town this morning to pick up some new work boots so I bought a few cans of black spray from pound land of all places!

After getting back I tried it on the wheel on the Landy and was impressed with the way it looked!

I then got the rest of the wheels out and gave them all a couple of coats.

Im am going to go with a black bumper front and back but that will have to be next week when I get the chance to get back to town on some errand Im sure the wife will have for me and buy some more spray!

Landy Project Costs

Land Rover £375

Sanding Discs £11.70

Ignition Barrel £20

Heritage letter £21.75

2x Batteries and rear 1/4 light £35

Pair Battery Terminal Clamps £3.99

Floor pan nuts & bolts £6.50

Grinding disc £2.25

Under Seal £8.99

Complete set of lights £85

5 Litres Primer £24.99

4 Discovery Wheels £10.20

Rear Door £21.00

Front Door £20.00

Handbrake spring £1.50

2 Discovery wheels

Two seatbelts

Wing Mirror

2 Headlight surrounds

2 headlight frames £60

2 Front Doors £60

Nato Green Paint £36

Rear Window Seal and insert £9.99

Wiring connectors £3.00

2 tins of silver metal paint £7.00

Fuses & Sandpaper £4.50

5x tins black spray £5.00

TOTAL £832.36

boguing

Re: The project has landed!

I think that you've made a good choice. I did my SIII wheels black. My kids agreed.

min200

Re: The project has landed!

Yea I considered green as well but black just seemed to fit the bill so much better.

min200

Re: The project has landed!

LMAO nope I want to actually use mine ;)

min200

Re: The project has landed!

Bumpers & Brakes
Main
Posted by min200 Wed, August 20, 2014 17:59:40

Today is the first day of six days off and I don't have to go on holiday with the Wife and kids or do anything in particular in fact I am just going to please my bloody self until I am told to do differently. The best thing is Wifey is at work until the weekend so I really do have a few days to myself!

Following on from blacking up the wheels I thought I would spray the bumpers black as well. So after a trip to the shops to buy some more paint I set to cleaning down and spraying up the front bumper....and it rained.

Not to be put off or have a bit of water ruin my good holiday mood I thought outside of the box and painted it in the greenhouse! The veg might taste a bit well paintish but that's just the new type of veg I am growing.

As I looked at the rear bumperettes I decided that spraying them in situ was a bad idea as there was a bit of a breeze and quite frankly I couldn't be arsed to take them off just to change the colour so I headed for a nose around in the shed. I came up with some black hammerite that was abandoned at the back of a shelf and there was just enough to give three good coats.
They have come out quite well. I did look at the Nato hitch but I am pretty sure that I am going to change it for a ball so I can drag a shed behind me when we go away for off road weekends so it was given a miss this time around.

By now the front bumper had dried so I set to digging out the new bolts and offering it up to the Landy. I remember it being a pain to get off and because it has a bit of a bend in it the nearside did take some "adjusting" with a hammer and pair of grips to get it on right. Then of course the bolts wouldn't drop down but after a couple of scuffed knuckles and some choice language from me they went in.

Then came fitting the washers and the nuts. For this may I

recommend bribing a small child to put them on because if you have fingers the size of sausages like myself you have no hope! In the end, and I am being serious here, I had to balance the nut and washer on the end of the ring spanner then feed t into the gap and try to get the threads to bite. So back to choice words and more blood but they all eventually went on and the results look better than I thought they would.

At this point in the proceedings I decided I wanted a roast dinner and a cup of tea so I took half an hour off to get all of that in motion because I AM on holiday and whats wrong with a Wednesday roast?

Then onto the brake system. If you remember I had some luck with the transmission brake but I didn't hold my breath on that luck lasting. Todays job was just to free off all of the brake adjusters so in I went with the WD40 and to my surprise I had the right imperial spanner for the adjuster 1/2.

On the front drums the adjuster was toward the bottom of the back plate and they both just freed off and started moving winding the pads back nicely.
On the back drums the adjuster is toward the upper part of the back plate.
I jacked up each end to make sure the wheels/drums moved freely enough ready for a strip down inspection.

The inspection will be later on as there is also a problem with the servo or master cylinder.
I then changed a few of the old fuses for new ones and I have a few spares if you need any seeing as I bpught in bulk to save cash!
That will do for today because the roast is nearly done and it smells gorgeous!!

Freetime101

Re: The project has landed!

Looking good, I think you may have 2 adusters on the fronts though. They look like TLS (twin leading shoe) so you'll have an adjuster for each shoe.

Can't believe how little you've spent vs how good it looks - I'm well jealous :)

min200

Re: The project has landed!

Quote:

Originally Posted by Freetime101 (Post 3187702)
Looking good, I think you may have 2 adusters on the fronts though. They look like TLS (twin leading shoe) so you'll have an adjuster for each shoe.

Can't believe how little you've spent vs how good it looks - I'm we jealous :)

Yet another valuable piece of advice thanks chap :) I shall investigate further!
I think the money will soon be mounting up as we get into the mechanics of it.....

min200

Re: The project has landed!

Quote:

> Originally Posted by easye1 (Post 3187592)
> *good work matey as usual....*

Thanks fella I do keep trying...or I am trying according to the Governor of the house ;)

min200

Re: The project has landed!

Leaks and Clutch
Main
Posted by min200 Thu, August 21, 2014 20:02:33

I awoke this morning feeling bloody great as it is yet another day off and Wifey then walked in with a cup of tea informing me both she and my daughters were off to her sisters for dinner this evening, apparently its a weekly thing they do, so I would be by myself doing as I please...heaven!

Well I didn't get off that easily as my youngest wanted to go swimming this morning but hey ho life is about memories eh so we jumped on our mountain bikes and went off for a couple of hours.

When I returned it was straight into shabby work gear and into the shed digging out the clutch master and slave cylinders and off to the Landy were I found this rather large leak...

It's coming from straight above it were the shaft goes into the transfer box...I think? Would one of you knowledgeable please tell me what it is and what seal needs replacing please and how to do it, in fact you may as well just pop over and fix it for me. yea a long shot I know so just the info would be a big help ;)

So I chucked some sand over it and popped an oil tray under it and left it to its own devices for now.

Onto the clutch I headed and the first job was to get the clutch pedal and master cylinder housing out.
I unscrewed the pipe work that goes to the slave cylinder first using the 1/2 spanner.
Then I had to undo the six bolts from inside the Landy running along the bulkhead next to the clutch pedal to release the framework.

After a bit of twisting around wiring brake pipes and the such the whole thing came out with the usual Land Rover sacrifice of some skin blood and choice language.
I then undid the two bolts holding the master cylinder onto the framework and it was ready for the new one to be fitted. I nearly forgot to remove the pipework coupling housing to put on the new one but noticed it was still on just as I was throwing it into the wheely bin so that saved a scramble through week old food to find it again!

While the framework was out I gave it a quick rub down and a spray up in the handy black paint.
The I refitted it all and went onto the slave cylinder.
If you have never had to fit a clutch slave cylinder to your motor be thankful to whatever god you pray to! What a ballache of a job it is!
The best way was to jack up the front onto axle stands then try to get yourself and tools into the tiny gap on the passenger side behind the exhaust and on top of the chassis. Sounds easy eh!

I first took off the pipework whilst trying to keep the falling rust out of my eyes and the clutch fluid from running too far up my arms!
Then I removed the bottom bolt holding the slave in...BIG mistake.
Because the slave was seized it then pushed up on the top bolt whilst

you were trying to remove that making it impossible to keep the socket in place so I attached some thin rope and pulled the cylinder back down refitting the bottom bolt.

Then I removed the top bolt first followed by the bottom with no problems. Whilst doing my Houdini impression I fitted the slave but then the pipe coupling would not screw into it for love nor money so after ten minutes I crawled out and made a brew. I decided it had to be a thread issue of course and took a torch back with me and a very thin screwdriver. Sure enough the thread on the coupling was ever so slightly bent just after the first turn so I carefully straightened it out with the screwdriver and it popped straight in first time.
Then came the bleeding. Well long story short it didn't really want to so after an hour of pumping pedals I remembered someone saying about reverse bleeding from the slave up with the old fashioned oil cans so I gave that a go with my eldest daughter watching the reservoir for bubbles and levels. She says there was air and I managed to stop it from overflowing as well which was nice.

There is now pressure on the clutch pedal but also some play and no amount of fannying about seems to change it But the gears do now engage. I havnt had the engine running but the wheels are off of the ground and they lock nicely when a gear is selected.

The exhaust was also retightened because I really want to get the engine running again this weekend to see if the clutch is working properly and the last time I started it it sounded like a Lancaster bomber!

So again another good day on the Landy and if it drives I think I may just pee myself with excitement just a little.

Landy Project Costs

Land Rover £375

Sanding Discs £11.70

Ignition Barrel £20

Heritage letter £21.75

2x Batteries and rear 1/4 light £35

Pair Battery Terminal Clamps £3.99

Floor pan nuts & bolts £6.50

Grinding disc £2.25

Under Seal £8.99

Complete set of lights £85

5 Litres Primer £24.99

4 Discovery Wheels £10.20

Rear Door £21.00

Front Door £20.00

Handbrake spring £1.50

2 Discovery wheels

Two seatbelts

Wing Mirror

2 Headlight surrounds

2 headlight frames £60

2 Front Doors £60

Nato Green Paint £36

Rear Window Seal and insert £9.99

Wiring connectors £3.00

2 tins of silver metal paint £7.00

Fuses & Sandpaper £4.50

5x tins black spray £5.00

5x more tins black spray £5.00

Clutch fluid

Exhaust putty

WD40 £8.49

TOTAL £845.85

Little Butch

Re: The project has landed!

I've just had my slave cylinder replaced at the garage... Glad I didn't do it myself now! :D
Good work though.

I need to do SOMETHING to mine today! Tempted to paint the disco wheels...

min200

Re: The project has landed!

Quote:

> Originally Posted by Little Butch (Post 3189066)
> *I've just had my slave cylinder replaced at the garage... Glad I didn't do it myself now! :D*
> *Good work though.*
>
> *I need to do SOMETHING to mine today! Tempted to paint the disco wheels...*

Go on get the paint out you know you want to!

Little Butch

Re: The project has landed!

That's what I need... Motivation! :D
Buuuuuut I changed my mind and bought a pressurised sprayer so I can change my gearbox oil, really needed doing!

min200

Re: The project has landed!

See you ended up doing a harder job I should start charging for motivational talks :D:D:D

Saying that I should get out there now I have finished my chores for the day and do something as well!

Little Butch

Re: The project has landed!

Haha! Yeah too bloody hard, I can't get the main drain plug undone, seems seized solid and I've only got a large adjustable instead of the 32mm spanner I need :/ haven't got a tube wide enough to slot over the adjustable either!

min200

Re: The project has landed!

Bugger.

dieselreek

Re: The project has landed!

Quote:

> Originally Posted by Little Butch (Post 3189203)
> *Haha! Yeah too bloody hard, I can't get the main drain plug undone, seems seized solid and I've only got a large adjustable instead of the 32mm spanner I need :/ haven't got a tube wide enough to slot over the adjustable either!*

try flattening the largest bit of pipe you have, make it fit

min200

Re: The project has landed!

Car Boot.
Main
Posted by min200 Sun, August 24, 2014 18:22:26

I like a car boot sale I have to admit. I love wandering around looking at what tat folk are selling and I love it even more when its tat I want to buy.

After a day off roading yesterday with the Nottingham Land Rover Club, who are a rather nice bunch of people that all have a laugh and took me and Wifey around the course all day, I realised there were to be many bits I needed to pick up for when my Landy is finally on the road.

With these and other bits in mind myself and Wifey wandered off to Tansley car boot in Derbyshire as we had wanted to before but never had the time. With it being a Bank holiday weekend the site was massive with loads of sellers so I thought there must be some pickings for me here. I was right! As I meandered about I came across a Jerry can that needs a bit of a refurb but still in great condition, a D ring, two snatch straps, around 18 metal grinding discs, cable ties, two small straps to hold the jerry can in place and a brand new padlock and keys to put on the Landy front spare wheel.

Now I like to haggle for a bargain but the prices started off reasonable so of course I haggled harder! The grand total for this collection of very useful bits...

£13 quid.

I know £13! Man I have had a good day today :)

Landy Project Costs

Land Rover £375

Sanding Discs £11.70

Ignition Barrel £20

Heritage letter £21.75

2x Batteries and rear 1/4 light £35

Pair Battery Terminal Clamps £3.99

Floor pan nuts & bolts £6.50

Grinding disc £2.25

Under Seal £8.99

Complete set of lights £85

5 Litres Primer £24.99

4 Discovery Wheels £10.20

Rear Door £21.00

Front Door £20.00

Handbrake spring £1.50

2 Discovery wheels

Two seatbelts

Wing Mirror

2 Headlight surrounds

2 headlight frames £60

2 Front Doors £60

Nato Green Paint £36

Rear Window Seal and insert £9.99

Wiring connectors £3.00

2 tins of silver metal paint £7.00

Fuses & Sandpaper £4.50

5x tins black spray £5.00

5x more tins black spray £5.00

Clutch fluid

Exhaust putty

WD40 £8.49

Car Boot Bits £13

TOTAL £858.85

easye1

Re: The project has landed!

lol.....

good man....

a days excorsize was worthwhile then :)

darius

Re: The project has landed!

Quote:

> Originally Posted by easye1 (Post 3191548)
> *lol.....*
>
> *good man....*
>
> *a days excorsize was worthwhile then :)*

exercise

min200

Re: The project has landed!

Quote:

Originally Posted by easye1 (Post 3191548)
lol.....

good man....

a days excorsize was worthwhile then :)

It was indeed! AND I got given another set of axle stands when I got home so the Landy is in the ait front and back now! Should make finishing the clutch bleed and brake rebuild a bit easier ;)

min200

Re: The project has landed!

Selling bits.
Main
Posted by min200 Mon, August 25, 2014 20:34:15

Digging around in my shed last week I came across the Military lights that I took off of the Landy as well as some old bike brake pads that

I bought many moons ago so I thought I may as well chuck them on fleabay to see what happens.

It amazes me that folk will pay more for second hand parts, the lights, because they are original than what they would cost to buy a newer replacement copy set. Those old rusty lights and I do not lie on my descriptions they were listed as rusty and replaced went for £41 to a chap in Italy who then had to pay £20 to have them posted!

I know they are original and I do get the point of when restoring a vehicle you would like to use as many original bits as you can but bugger me its going to cost over £100 all in with the repairs that need doing to those light frames and bowls which is a price way to steep for a tight arse like me!

The bike brake pads went for £15 as well so I put the money to good use buying replacement shocks for the old Landy. Cheaper end shocks admittedly but far better than the rusty crap that's already on the old girl and perfectly priced for a miserly git like me.

Maybe I should pop them on Ebay when they are changed over to see if anyone wants to buy them?

Landy Project Costs

Land Rover £375

Sanding Discs £11.70

Ignition Barrel £20

Heritage letter £21.75

2x Batteries and rear 1/4 light £35

Pair Battery Terminal Clamps £3.99

Floor pan nuts & bolts £6.50

Grinding disc £2.25

Under Seal £8.99

Complete set of lights £85

5 Litres Primer £24.99

4 Discovery Wheels £10.20

Rear Door £21.00

Front Door £20.00

Handbrake spring £1.50

2 Discovery wheels

Two seatbelts

Wing Mirror

2 Headlight surrounds

2 headlight frames £60

2 Front Doors £60

Nato Green Paint £36

Rear Window Seal and insert £9.99

Wiring connectors £3.00

2 tins of silver metal paint £7.00

Fuses & Sandpaper £4.50

5x tins black spray £5.00

5x more tins black spray £5.00

Clutch fluid

Exhaust putty

WD40 £8.49

Car Boot Bits £13

Front & rear shocks £59.45

TOTAL £918.30

easye1 25th-August-2014 23:40

Re: The project has landed!

Quote:

Originally Posted by darius (Post 3191651)
exercise

well feck me, someone who can spell..........
now, thats a first for landyzone eh.........................#### :D

Brown

Re: The project has landed!

Well, maybe it did need exorcising. It could have been haunted. It'll be much better when the unquiet spirit has departed.

min200

Re: The project has landed!

Finishing the clutch
Main
Posted by min200 Fri, August 29, 2014 10:51:54

A change in work hours has put a stop to yet more of the pottering enjoyment of life but hey the plus side is that I get to see Wifey a bit more during the week...apparently.

But today I arose from my slumber a little earlier so went and got the swimming training out of the way with all of the sporty set at the local pool rather than the old gits I normally have a paddle with. You wouldn't think that there would be a designer war on how to look good when walking along the poolside to get in but it seems there is.

These "Sporty" clowns have the most expensive budgie smugglers that money can buy along with reflective tinted swimming goggles. I mean why would you need reflective bloody swimming goggles in an indoor pool?? I just smirked to myself and got my 40 lengths in and walked off in a strutting manor posing my £3.99 shorts form Tesco.

So after getting home and dragging the dog out for a quick walk I set to getting the Landy started again to see if the clutch would engage seeing as there seemed to be so much play in it. Of course the old wreck wouldn't start and upon further inspection it seemed all of the fuel had run back into the tanks so I suppose there is a hole somewhere in the fuel lines or fuel pump gaskets that needs sorting but I am not going to bugger about with it for about £50 I am just going to replace the lot and be done with it!

I have been toying with changing over to a single fuel tank instead of the twins ones so maybe its a sign to just get on with it.

I managed to get the fuel back through and the engine running and to my happiness and amazement the clutch engages perfectly fine and the wheel spin nicely so that's a plus for the day. The axles will want a good service as well as the gear & transfer box but I will get to these eventually.

I then set to the clutch pedal as there was about 3" of movement before pressure and I started with the Haynes manual for a quick read and it pointed me in the direction of a nut on the outside of the master cylinder cage.
Literally a couple of turns in and it sorted the pedal play right out! So the clutch now works and the pedal feels like it should do.

So for a spare hour not a bad amount done and with this coming Monday off and Wifey at work providing the weather holds it should be a playing day!

Little Butch

29th-August-2014 11:01

Re: The project has landed!

My defenders got a bit of play in the clutch, wonder of this is possible on a defender? I'll have to have a gander :D
I've run outta money so am stuck not being able to do a lot to mine... Bored!

min200

29th-August-2014 11:18

Re: The project has landed!

Sucks when the cash runs dry!!!

Little Butch

29th-August-2014 11:56

Re: The project has landed!

Sure does! I've taken to removing all the lights and spraying the connectors with wd40... Shows how bored I am haha! You got a rough idea of when this will be on the road mate?

min200

Re: The project has landed!

Got to get those connections rust proof! as for completion next weekend would be good but in reality I think it should be around March time if the weather isn't too bad over winter.

Brown

Re: The project has landed!

Still, you've got as cracking machine on a really tight budget. I never realised Land Rover motoring could be so wallet-friendly. This thread has been an education.

min200

Re: The project has landed!

Thanks for that :) Im a tight arsed git who doesn't like parting with my hard earned cash you know lol

Nah really I just trawl through websites looking for bargains and I have been lucky with the condition of the Landy underneath the state it was in when I bought it. My aim is to have it done on a £1500 budget but we shall see what the mechanics of it are like and the costs they may bring!

min200

Re: The project has landed!

Landy Project Costs

Land Rover £375

Sanding Discs £11.70

Ignition Barrel £20

Heritage letter £21.75

2x Batteries and rear 1/4 light £35

Pair Battery Terminal Clamps £3.99

Floor pan nuts & bolts £6.50

Grinding disc £2.25

Under Seal £8.99

Complete set of lights £85

5 Litres Primer £24.99

4 Discovery Wheels £10.20

Rear Door £21.00

Front Door £20.00

Handbrake spring £1.50

2 Discovery wheels

Two seatbelts

Wing Mirror

2 Headlight surrounds

2 headlight frames £60

2 Front Doors £60

Nato Green Paint £36

Rear Window Seal and insert £9.99

Wiring connectors £3.00

2 tins of silver metal paint £7.00

Fuses & Sandpaper £4.50

5x tins black spray £5.00

5x more tins black spray £5.00

Clutch fluid

Exhaust putty

WD40 £8.49

Car Boot Bits £13

Front & rear shocks £59.45

Front & rear brake rebuild kits £81.62

TOTAL £999.92

boguing
1st-September-2014 22:22

Re: The project has landed!

I do enjoy your writing!

min200
1st-September-2014 23:15

Re: The project has landed!

Quote:

> Originally Posted by boguing (Post 3200507)
> *I do enjoy your writing!*

Thanks I enjoy doing it! This was the second draft because after I had written about three quarters of it the first time my bloody Bearded dragon decided to do a dance on the keyboard and closed the web browser down loosing the lot!

I did consider making some Dragon skin boots out of him but he just looked at me tasted the keyboard sort of smirked and shot off again towars his Viv. So he gets to live another day that and the fact he's the only other bloke in the house even the dog is a bitch ;)

Brown
2nd-September-2014 00:47

Re: The project has landed!

Looks like the brake bits are the most expensive item, aside from the Land Rover itself. Still, it's worth doing as it is all safety critical. I replaced all my seals, pistons, flexible hoses and some of the metal pipes last year and I just feel so much more at ease driving around now, knowing that it is all nice new stuff and that I've put it together properly.

min200
2nd-September-2014 07:33

Re: The project has landed!

That's it isn't it and I still need to spend another £50-£60 on new hoses pipes etc and if the servo is fubar another £60 on top of that! BUT having said that I would rather do them right and they should last me a few years then.

Re: The project has landed!

back lights and Birthdays
Main
Posted by min200 Tue, September 02, 2014 09:20:33

Have you seen the weather out there today? It's glorious! The sun is shining in a clear blue cloudless sky. Can you imagine having this sort of day to do as you please no work a days holiday booked, I can imagine it and I can also tick most of those boxes but my there is some fuss on in the house today because my eldest daughter is turning 18.

You would think that it was an important event the way they are all going in this house and the fuss that is coming form me posting this picture on her facebook page is unbelievable!

There should be a really funny picture here but my eldest daughter threatened to sue me if it went to print as well as online so I wont publish it here...but f you do want to see it go straight to nickysmith.me and look there ;)
Cant see what the fuss is about myself?

Anyway the best thing about today is that the women in my household do like a lie in when they get the chance (lazy gits really) so I walked the dog and then got stuck into having a look at my number plate light housing. The old one was a bit broken and rusty.

First I had to remove the protective cover cunningly held on by a single 8mm nut

This exposed the back of the old housing so a quick turn of a couple of nuts and its off with the old then on with the new part. I did think about replacing this with a genuine Land Rover part but after costing it all up and deciding that that small mortgage could wait for another day I "acquired" the bit I fitted from a mechanic friend for the price of a cup of tea...that I made with his stuff ;)

I did have to drill a new hole but hey that's a small price to pay for saving some cash. just need to fill a little hole and touch up the paint work and all is good.
Well apparently we are going out for brunch I have just been told and there is some threat of shopping going on as well god help me. Why oh why could I not have had a whole brood of sons?

min200

6th-September-2014 20:24

Re: The project has landed!

Do I line them up?
Main
Posted by min200 Sat, September 06, 2014 20:23:31

I am in a bit of a quandary this evening. One Land Rover does always lead to another BUT I didn't think it would happen this soon. There is maybe an opportunity to acquire an 88" model as well at a good price that would need nothing more than a few hours work to get back onto the road.
This would have me charging around off road this side of Christmas and leave the 109" on the drive for a more leisurely rebuild...
Oh what to do?

Come on folks throw a little advice my way here!

Little Butch
7th-September-2014 11:07

Re: The project has landed!

Buy it! :D

Iann
7th-September-2014 14:12

Re: The project has landed!

Buy it :D

Discovery2TD5
7th-September-2014 14:21

The project has landed!

You can never have too many Land Rovers.
Especially series ones at that.

min200
7th-September-2014 19:42

Re: The project has landed!

Well I missed out on it anyway :(
But then someone has told me about another 109 so maybe there
will be another lol

aaronmorris

Re: The project has landed!

> Quote:
>
> Originally Posted by min200 (Post 3207521)
> *Well I missed out on it anyway :(*
> *But then someone has told me about another 109 so maybe there*
> *will be another lol*

Yes, Because 1 Landrover is just never enough :D

easye1

Re: The project has landed!

well, firstly, belated birthday wished to your daughter...
my eldist girl is twice yours age, with another not far behind.
my sanity (oh rearly) is held together by my "little boy"
hes 44 now........lol
he leads me astray on all things motor scooter and aircooled VW`s..

ok, yep, you have the landy bug big time now my friend..

min200

Re: The project has landed!

Not alot doing.
Main
Posted by min200 Tue, September 09, 2014 08:42:17

I haven't really had a chance to do much this past week because of the way the wonderful new shift pattern falls at work to include Saturdays. This shift pattern is so good it is already failing leaving trunks with no drivers at all times of the day and we did point this out before it was implemented but we were just "moaning drivers who don't like change".

Don't get me wrong we are moaning drivers and we don't like any sort of change especially if it includes making us work weekends but we are not thick and we can see what's in front of our faces even if the kids fresh out of Uni with a bit of paper that says they are transport managers cannot. Bless em 22 years old and know it all, they can't drive a truck everywhere is half an inch away on a map "Birmingham to Carlise only an hour or so" and still struggle to find their own asses whilst Mummy does their washing because they still live at home with mounting students debts BUT we drivers are the thickos with no idea...you have to laugh!

Still enough moaning I have had a chance to spray up the old Jerry can I bought in my greenhouse because I don't have a nice spraybooth to hand.

It's come up quite well I think. I did consider using some of my left over nato green paint but then found out I did have any paint brushes so a black spray can that was kicking around it was!

Land Rovers are like buses and I have been offered two more in the last few days but after much thinking and worrying and cursing to myself I decided to buy one. The first an 88" had been sold and the second a 109" was in being stored in Lancaster so that put an end to that. For the best really as I have come too far with this old motor to get distracted now!

I'm making a list of parts I need for the Land Rover Show in Peterborough in a week or so and the primary bits will be the rest of the brake system rebuild along with a couple of nice defender seats that I will find for a tenner....oh no that was a dream I had last night.

A weekend off is looming so hopefully I can get a bit of the brake rebuild started.

easye1

Re: The project has landed!

happy birthday for just being 40 - a milestone....

thinking back 40 years (how long) is when I bought a brand new yamaha DT175.
was working days, lived on the very outskirts of north romford and could ride half way to work through forest and open common land....
was just 26 years old then, and raced mini rods - min ;)
thinking back even more, I could fit in them then too, and get in & out through the glass less window holes ala General Lee style..

have a problem getting in any car at the mo, got a leg that dont like bending - such is life..

min200

Re: The project has landed!

I turned 40 last year but just called the blog it when I first bought the webspace...thought it had a nice ring to it ;)

The big 41 is fast approaching but hell age really is just a number and it took me some time to get that through my midlife crisis!

Time to live well and we do do that now. There is always something to do at the weekend and there is so much to see! 26 years old...just a memory now lol

min200

Re: The project has landed!

Postage & Steering
Main
Posted by min200 Sat, September 13, 2014 17:54:54

I love the internet. I love being able to hop on it and order what I need knowing it will turn up a couple of days later and I have not had to drive around to a few different places talking to teenage pleb ends who have no interest in what I want to buy or in giving the correct product let alone the time of day.

I do try and box clever with delivery though. I order stuff aiming for it to arrive when I am around the house to save that nightmare trip to the local sorting office to be met by a grown up pleb who will not be able to find my parcel amongst the piles of them they have hidden out of eyesight in these places.

My family don't share the same view on delivery they just order their crap normally from the other side of the world and then miss the delivery and moan like bloody hell until they have it in their hands and promptly forget about the tat they have bought in a couple of hours. My eldest daughter has done just that. She missed a parcel she just "HAD" to have today but she was at work all morning and the sorting office would be closed when she was done so the inevitable "Daaaadd" came out and I was forced to go and pick the bloody thing up this morning.

The thing is I had ordered a tank bag for the motorbike as I would need it for the charity week that's fast approaching and I had to collect some bits for the Landy this morning but "no great panic" I thought to myself as Wifey and the youngest will be in while I am out so all they have to do is answer the door and take it off of the postman.

No great task that is it?

Well I picked up a replacement fuel tank along with the funnel fittings and a set of steering bars then headed for the sorting office. All was going well and I was making good time until I arrived there. There were a few folk queuing all the way down the side of the building of course so my marathon 45 minute wait for a parcel I didn't want or need started. The one single pleb serving seemed to be illiterate which is a handy trait a post office building and seemed to look at pictures on his phone more than peoples collection cards. Stating my annoyance in a civil manner of course is probably why he took 5 minutes to have a cup of tea/collect my daughters parcel but

I had it soon enough and escaped home to find a big red parcel collection note on my front door mat and my wonderful family still snoring in bed.

They still wonder why I am pissed off! Back to the sorting office pleb on Monday morning for my tank bag it is then.

Still I had the chance of a couple of hours on the project today so firstly I had to spray up the new steering bars ready for fitting as the rust colour wasn't that fetching.
Then I cleaned up and sealed the replacement fuel tank.

The reason for changing from twin tanks to a single is because I want a filler neck. The idea of taking out both seat bases when I fuel up really is unappealing so while I am doing the rebuild of the fuel system which was everything but the fuel tank a little extra work is not a problem.

Then it was onto the steering bars. The original ones were banana shaped and god only knows how they ended up that way! I can only presume some monkey decided to strap it up on them or lift them with a fork lift!

The bends were pretty severe so much so the front wheels were facing inwards. The smaller bar came off easy enough but the longer bar decided it had to have the usual blood and pain sacrifice to the Landy gods before giving up.

One set of the replacement track rod ends were in reqally good condition but I will need to replace the ones on the longer bar but I have fitted the bar into place to keep everything in the right order and nit confuse myself!

They look well though and yes I know I am sad liking how my new steering bars.

The wheels are straight now which is nice! I managed to swap these bars for an old wing skin I had kicking around which is always better than having to pay for them!

Of course then the Wife started shouting about how I had to get clean because we have to go and do something dull somewhere else so the tools were packed away and I took solace in the mental list I have of whats left to do.

I have just realised that my costing list has not taken into account the refunds of money for the bits I have sold off of the Landy. I shall tot up what I have made and then add it as a credit to the costing's

Landy Project Costs

Land Rover £375

Sanding Discs £11.70

Ignition Barrel £20

Heritage letter £21.75

2x Batteries and rear 1/4 light £35

Pair Battery Terminal Clamps £3.99

Floor pan nuts & bolts £6.50

Grinding disc £2.25

Under Seal £8.99

Complete set of lights £85

5 Litres Primer £24.99

4 Discovery Wheels £10.20

Rear Door £21.00

Front Door £20.00

Handbrake spring £1.50

2 Discovery wheels

Two seatbelts

Wing Mirror

2 Headlight surrounds

2 headlight frames £60

2 Front Doors £60

Nato Green Paint £36

Rear Window Seal and insert £9.99

Wiring connectors £3.00

2 tins of silver metal paint £7.00

Fuses & Sandpaper £4.50

5x tins black spray £5.00

5x more tins black spray £5.00

Clutch fluid

Exhaust putty

WD40 £8.49

Car Boot Bits £13

Front & rear shocks £59.45

Front & rear brake rebuild kits £81.62

Fuel tank & filler £40

TOTAL £1039.92

min200

14th-September-2014 18:00

Re: The project has landed!

Sickness sunshine & shock absorbers
Main
Posted by min200 Sun, September 14, 2014 17:54:55

A full weekend off is a rare treat these days as work in the modern world takes no distinction from the days of the week.

Our plans for the day were to head off into Derbyshire on the motorbike as we were kid free as well for a change which gives us a chance to be Nick & Lian again instead of Muuuum and Daaad but as I opened my eyes I knew that Autumn was coming and long with it a batch of new bugs to have a go at the system.

I felt like someone had removed me from my slumber during the night taking me outside placing me in the middle of the road just in time for the nearest bus to hit me.

Sore throat sick stomach and a pounding head...not a good mix for a day on the bike. Wifey soon awoke as well complaining of the same and I knew she must be ill because she was awake and up before 9am on a weekend day off.

I am not one for sitting about and feeling sorry for myself when a bug hits home in fact I have dragged myself to work more than once when feeling bad only to be turned around as soon as I got there by the staff quoting some health and safety bull about driving when you look like crap! so seeing as the sun was out and the kids had done a fine job of buggering off we popped out to a car boot sale where I picked up a towball, bottle jack and a water container for the Landy for the grand sum on £5.40. Should be useful on trips out!

When we got home Wifey collapsed on the sofa and I have to say I was tempted to join her but the weather was good and I thought a potter on the project was a good idea. I decided to see how hard it was to sort the shock absorbers.

The front ones were pretty rusty..
I set to taking the split pin out which came ok considering how long its been there and was still in a usable condition. The top bolts came out no bother at all.

Now folk have been telling me that when you fit a new front shock its a bitch to get the pin back in because the new rubbers need compressing so much and the ideas and tools folk had made made the mind boggle!

I found it was just easy to first clamp on side down with a g clamp tp put the pin in and then clamp the other side and push the split pin through.
Looks better with the new shock in place :)
I was still feeling ok-ish so I tackeled the other side as well!

Then onto the back ones. These were a bit more of a pain because the rust was so bad on the back ones.
I ended up having to grind them off but please take note here and be mindful of the axle straps because if you don't you will end up having to buy new ones because you have cut through your old ones!
I fitted the new shock no bother and again it looks good under there :)

I did the other side to but I then admitted defeat to the bugs in my body. The rest of the day will be spent eating chocolate drinking tea and maybe a strong bit of something medicinal later on this evening.

easye1   14th-September-2014 20:22

Re: The project has landed!

does 1988 have a ring to it.... lol
I was 40 then.
think my midlife crisis came home in the 1970`s via small oval racing.
a brand new DT175 came in 1974 too, as I could cut my work

journey in half by riding through a forest & common land....
never got caught, but did get shouted at by a horse rider (legal yamaha) ??
the DT`s love affair lasted 3 years until I sold it.
My small oval racing lasted till 1986 until a banger world final in a mk1 granada that was a gutless 2 1/2 litre piece of shite where I sat and thought as I urged the thing to go faster but unsucesful - doing the laps I just thought --- WTF am I doing here or wtf am I doing with my life.....at that point and the end of that race, I loaded up, went home, put the almost undented grannie away, and never went back to it nor the other two garages full of my racing gear - gone - finished......
I then turned full bore into work - work and more work....
LOL....
that lasted till my (propper job) nightwork running two HM3 machining centres poping out bits that flew - but the job flew instead via Insolvency..
I then thought - yep - WTF am I doing now....lol
a 55yo, fully trained in aerospace componant production, able to operate and run any machine shop equipement - but no job - nor no pay - nor no chance to sign on or claim a penny from the gov.com as my dear mrs was working her socks of too..
WTF to do.....
year later - big house sold - tiny seaside home purchased outright, said boll*x to it all and we (me & mrs) both retired 10 years early..
money was tight, we got through, our hard earned state pensions kicked in...
happy days....

So, my "mid life crisis" turned out much longer than yours, but its been a fun roller coaster all along the way.

appollogies for spelling - length of drivel - living so long - but being a LZ member its my thing ;)

min200

Re: The project has landed!

Nor drivel and chat away! How can you live too long chap lol.

I love my life, don't get me wrong there is still a hell of a lot to do and I cannot wait to get out of this city but we have it good compared to many folk out there.

Count my blessings and all that!

The landy will be around for a long time and the next thing will be another motorbike!

min200

Re: The project has landed!

Shows Parts and Pennies
Main
Posted by min200 Sun, September 21, 2014 16:05:50

Excuse me if this gets a little disjointed the Wife is chewing my ear about some nonsense that A) doesn't effect me and B) I am not the slightest bit interested in but I must pretend I am listening and grunt in the right places or she will just talk for longer.

Yesterday was the Land Rover show at Peterborough and I have been looking forward to it. As a Land rover show "virgin" I was under the impression I would be able to buy all of the bits I needed to complete my little project and took enough money to do so after pricing the parts up online. How mistaken I was.

If you wanted to buy a winch bumper or spend a small fortune on a flashy interior that was the place to go. If you wanted to pay more than new prices for old bits of scrap at the auto jumble stores this was the place for you! I mean one bloke tried to charge me £30 for a series indicator stalk....THIRTY BLOODY QUID for a £12 part???? yea ok mate would you like my pin number as well in fact have the wife while you are at it!

Now don't get me wrong it was great looking at all the different motors I was quite in my element with that but going for the normal rebuild parts is obviously a bad idea and now I know so next year I shall go prepared and buy a winch bumper.
Anyway when I got home I jumped online and ordered loads of new bits in fact enough bits to hopefully finish the Landy off apart from anything the axles need and front seats.

I then found an old advert for 24v bits near my parents place so I called and bought all manner of bits off of the chap including a rear bench seat so something else ticked off of the list.

Then there was the wheels. You know I spent ages deciding what colour to paint my wheels and ended up with black which was all nice and good now only needing new tyres. I found some tyres. They were really good tyres. They were on the same rims as I had already done up so I am not going to be taking them off of one set to put them on the other same type of wheel set like was suggested by the wife who couldn't see the issue with spending the money to swap them over onto exactly the same wheels.

So she told me to paint them again.
But I am far too tight to go and buy more spray paint. Why would I when there is perfectly good NATO paint in the shed so I thought I would try that first and the results are pretty good even if I do say so

myself.
Bugger the black NATO green it is then!

The fuel system strip out was next on todays list so I jumped to it and it took all of 20 minutes to remove both tanks and the change over switch.

The Chassis had a quick rub down and was under sealed again. No pictures of it painted black you have seen all that before! I did clean up the twin tanks and they will be on Ebay later today along with the set of 5 steel disco wheels I no longer need!

There was one last buy at the Landy show that dear Wifey made me get. Apparently I am a bit of a git for wrecking clothes when working on the project so a babygrow was in order.
By babygrow I mean an old all in one flight suit...does the job though!
This way I am told I can wear what ever I want to work on it and never ruin anything but it doesn't matter that I look like I am about to pay some expensive hooker who deals in extreme fetishes a large amount of money.

I like a challenge.....

Landy Project Costs

Land Rover £375

Sanding Discs £11.70

Ignition Barrel £20

Heritage letter £21.75

2x Batteries and rear 1/4 light £35

Pair Battery Terminal Clamps £3.99

Floor pan nuts & bolts £6.50

Grinding disc £2.25

Under Seal £8.99

Complete set of lights £85

5 Litres Primer £24.99

4 Discovery Wheels £10.20

Rear Door £21.00

Front Door £20.00

Handbrake spring £1.50

2 Discovery wheels

Two seatbelts

Wing Mirror

2 Headlight surrounds

2 headlight frames £60

2 Front Doors £60

Nato Green Paint £36

Rear Window Seal and insert £9.99

Wiring connectors £3.00

2 tins of silver metal paint £7.00

Fuses & Sandpaper £4.50

5x tins black spray £5.00

5x more tins black spray £5.00

Clutch fluid

Exhaust putty

WD40 £8.49

Car Boot Bits £13

Front & rear shocks £59.45

Front & rear brake rebuild kits £81.62

Fuel tank & filler £40

Wheels complete with tyres £250

Fuel pump

Fuel hose

Indicator stalk

Bonnet strap

Brake switch

Fuel pump gasket

Fuel line clips £67.74

24v Wiper motor

24v flasher relay

24v heater

24v front loom

oil cooler

Door tops x2

Rear bench seat £67.50

TOTAL £1425.16

Mrtea

Re: The project has landed!

Is this the Landy I drive past on the ring road most mornings?

min200

Re: The project has landed!

I expect so if its between Mansfield Road and the City Hospital roundabout ;)

easye1

Re: The project has landed!

"This way I am told I can wear what ever I want to work on it and never ruin anything but it doesn't matter"
Ideal work gear mate..

finding one pair to fit my frame is a challenge ;)
so I make do with my "john boy" bib & brace overalls, and ruined T shirts on the shoulders..

min200

Re: The project has landed!

Yep I was supposed to wear "old clothes" but you know getting changed is just such ahrd work!

aaronmorris

Re: The project has landed!

Quote:

> Originally Posted by min200 (Post 3224056)
> *Yep I was supposed to wear "old clothes" but you know getting changed is just such ahrd work!*

I find I say "I'm just nipping out for 5 I wont get dirty"
Next thing I've been outside all day and my clothes are f*cked :o
So I now no longer have decent clothes and everything is "scruffs" Not like I go anywhere anyway.

min200

Re: The project has landed!

That's about the sum of it here as well chap lol
But the baby grow should put pay to that!

Mrtea

Re: The project has landed!

:D keep up the good work, cheers me up every time I see it on the way to work!!

min200

22nd-September-2014 19:57

Re: The project has landed!

Quote:

> Originally Posted by Mrtea (Post 3224786)
> *:D keep up the good work, cheers me up every time I see it on the way to work!!*

Well if you see me out on the drive working on it when you pass feel free to stop and have a nose at it and a brew :)

min200

27th-September-2014 18:57

Re: The project has landed!

Tanks and Switches
Main
Posted by min200 Sat, September 27, 2014 18:50:26

Have you ever been volunteered for a job at work and you think "yea why not it will make a change and a few extra quid" then as soon as you started doing that job thought "Why in Gods name did I say I would do this?" Well that's where I am at now.]

12 hours a day 6 days a week seemed like a great idea bringing in extra cash but the actual job is mind numbing as hell! Basically I am a traffic director whilst a massive area outside of the biggest warehouse we have is being re tarmacked so I get to argue with outside drivers that they cant park their trucks there and basically puch people around to keep the flow of trailers moving....I would rather be hung up by my pubic hair on the nearest light bulb than do the next two weeks I have left on it!

But there was a silver lining as we finished phase one within a couple hours of arriving at work this morning so I promptly ran off home before I could be found some other mind numbing chore for me to do by those folk in the offices that all they seem to do is compare job titles and measure each others dicks!

So onto the landy as soon as I got home with the unexpected extra time I had in the day. I decided on rebuilding the fuel system that I stripped out last time I had any time on the old girl. First was to remove the old fuel pump that was caked up with some sort of fuzz and cobwebs.
The fuel lines were brittle as hell so getting them out wasn't a problem.
Two bolts that hold the fuel pump on cam off easily and to my surprise there was no gasket behind it so it may of rotted away or not been there to start with but it made cleaning the face up for a good fit of the new pump easy.

I popped the pump on and then fitted new brake line front to back but discovered that the flexi hose that connects to the carb was perished but does it have to have that? Is it going to cause me any great problems without it? I shall be asking around to see but fitting it later wont be a problem.

Then it was onto fitting the 88" fuel tank. Apart from cutting a hole in the floor for the filler to come out of it wasn't really a problem apart from the fact that if you don't have a large high jack, two pairs of hands or the use of the force you will struggle to do this by yourself.

Having said that the lovely ladies of my home just looked at me like I had asked if they would clean the front driveway with their tongues when I asked for a helping hand so I went and dug out my big jack, my spare set of hands, quickly read up on my jedi mind powers and got stuck in. After 20 minutes of mild foul language dropping tools when I really could have done without doing so and a couple of trapped fingers later the tank was in.

I connected the fuel pipe then looked at the wiring from the twin tanks realising I had not marked or taken any notice of what two wires I would need to plug back in for the fuel gauge to work called myself a few derogatory names and added it to my list of what I must find out as well as finding out where the fuel filler cap should be so it works and connects to the tank as its supposed to.

After a quick tidy around, the driveway was starting to look like a jumble sale with tools and rubbish strewn all over the place, I decided to fit the new brake switch. It wasn't too hard but I did have to slacken off the top nuts on the brake servo in order to remove the old and fit the new brake switch.
After some fiddling around I actually got the brake lights to work! That's one set of lights on the rear of the motor that actually do!!

There was one troubling thing I did notice while crawling around under the landy and that was maybe a couple of bolts might be missing from what I think is the clutch housing...could be something else mind but Im learning as I go here but they are missing in the following pics if anyone can shed any light on it...

So another pleasant afternoon spent pottering about when I should have been working which has made it so much more enjoyable.

min200

Re: The project has landed!

What can you do in 5 mins?
Main

A proper day off today and as it turns out it was my wedding anniversary...whoops. Now luckily I was up very early because of the daft hours im working and downstairs I found a card from Wifey to me. Soooo I quickly headed out to "walk the dog" before she woke up and actually found a decnt bunch of flowers at the petrol station up the road along with a blank card to write in! I mean what are the odds of finding both at the local BP? talk about luck on my side!

So with Wifey happy when she woke up we headed off into Derbyshire to have a hunt around a carboot/market and lunch out in the park at Matlock. While we were sitting there it came to my attention what shite parenting goes on in the world. There was a women screaming at a two year old that he was a waste of space and needed to wlk faster, a Dad looking more at his phone while his kid was doing his best to drown himself in the river but the cream de le cream were the parents that were just smiling at their daughter who just kept screaming at the top of her voice and this was a scream that could break glass over a ten minute period because she wanted an ice cream.

Now when I was a kid I got a slap if I stood out of line, if my parents weren't there to do it any other adult that was kicking around would happily stand in and give you a slap if you were being a shit. I have slapped my own kids on the very rare occasion it has been needed and they have turned out to be ok with no mental scars but we seem to have the first generation that was raised without punishments for their actions now having their own kids whilst having no clue what to do to discipline them. Honestly it takes everything I have inme not to first walk up to the latest little shits and tell them off whilst slapping their parents at the same time.

Still enough of my griping Wifey decided she was going to hoover the car out so I had a window of twenty minutes to do something Landy related but what can you do in that time without getting filthy?

The answer is gators. Two gators one on the handbrake and one on the 4wd knob.
Easy enough to do just whip out the screws take off the old gators and refit!
The old gators were past their best!
Then the hoover went quiet so playtime was over. Next job will be to finish the fuel pipe cap bit on the bodywork at some point over the next couple of weeks.

easye1

28th-September-2014 20:50

Re: The project has landed!

funny you talk of hoovers.
when ever i do car works that makes mess, i have a little mains powered hand held hoover that has a flexi pipe....
great for hoovering out places your working in, or into hollow voids, or if you drop that last nut and cant reach it..
back when I was under my landy for months welding in my spare time, I used this hoover constantly..its little J cloth type collection bag just gets hand washed out if it gets oily
under or on a landy - it gets oily..

min200

4th-October-2014 17:46

Re: The project has landed!

Birthday Bonus
Main
Posted by min200 Sat, October 04, 2014 17:44:00
Well today is my birthday and its the big 4-1, perhaps I should now rename the blog just turned 41 but it really doesn't have the same ring to it.
Anyway I can hand on heart say it has, so far, been the best birthday I have had in years! A new laptop (how very extravagant!) proper ales in bottles, slippers and chocolate to put Thonton's to shame BUT there was on extra bonus that I had to pay for myself but it was worth it!
The last but best present was a full length roof rack with ladder for the Landy at a cost of £100 delivered!

The chaps who dropped it off helped me pop it onto the project as well which saved me some stress of trying to put it on myself and the results are pretty good as well!

That's all I can get in today as I need to get ready to be dragged out to a restaurant for a slap up meaty mal and a few real ales to boot. It's a dirty job but I will try to persevere!

easye1

Re: The project has landed!

happy birthday mate whenever you read this...
41 eh....

25 years ago to me ;)

min200

Re: The project has landed!

Quote:

Originally Posted by easye1 (Post 3237236)
happy birthday mate whenever you read this...
41 eh....

25 years ago to me ;)

Thanks for the birthday wishes old timer ;)

elan23

5th-October-2014 08:39

Re: The project has landed!

OK 1) 'missing bolt' is wading plug hole I think ie. don't worry.
2) I am building up the courage to start on my own 109 LWB exMOD so I follow your post with interest.
3) LRO magazine seem to be sorting an ex MOD 109, interesting but they could have made a much better journalistic job than they have (imho).

min200

5th-October-2014 15:07

Re: The project has landed!

Quote:

Originally Posted by elan23 (Post 3237635)
OK 1) 'missing bolt' is wading plug hole I think ie. don't worry.
2) I am building up the courage to start on my own 109 LWB exMOD so I follow your post with interest.
3) LRO magazine seem to be sorting an ex MOD 109, interesting but they could have made a much better journalistic job than they have (imho).

Yea I should have said I was told it was a wading plug hole and the plug itself is on the bracket just below it.

just get stuck in on your 109 who cares if you make the odd wrong turn just smile to yourself admit a lesson learnt and write online about it so everyone can have a laugh at your expense...oh wait no that was me lol

I may have to go and buy LRO and have a look at that then.

min200

Re: The project has landed!

Getting ready.
Main
Posted by min200 Sat, October 11, 2014 12:58:42

They say time flies and it really does in what seems like a blink of the eye I have arrived upon the eve of going away to The Outward Bound Trust in wales that I was raising money for a while back.

When they asked for volunteers it was on a nice spring day with the promise of a superb summer to follow so I said yes but has anyone else noticed it turned a bit bloody chilly this week and I will be spending most of next week either on a Welsh mountainside or in some sort of river bay or pond...

So this morning was spent buying the local Yeomans out of thermal under wear and woolly socks! Im looking forward to helping these kids out but im buggered if I will spend any more time than needs be being freezing cold and wet! Bought a few extra bits as well just in case the kids coming don't have the luxury of such things.

SO with this and the daft 12 hour days if the past few weeks the Landy has been a bit neglected with a pile of parts in the shed waiting to go on and a job left half finished but after next week I will have the time to dive back in and get a load more work done to it.

Give me a week and I will be boring the pants off of you all again after I have come home and defrosted first.

easye1   11th-October-2014 16:06

Re: The project has landed!

you go and have some fun lad, and the kids will remember you and it forever...

I too have stocked up on socks, today was "dickies boot socks" at Aldi, and in the week it was knee high arctic winter boot socks in wool/nylon mix from army surplus via ebay--- but they are really thick, sort of 3 sizes boots too big...must need wellies now to wear them with....:rolleyes:

min200   11th-October-2014 17:32

Re: The project has landed!

:) I like new socks! I have just sorted through the mounds of old ones I have while packing for the week and my word they needed replacing!

tyre man dave

Re: The project has landed!

just got a new project

need to sell my other two

min200

Re: The project has landed!

The Outward Bound Trust
Main
Posted by min200 Sun, October 19, 2014 14:14:21

Well I am back from my week away with the kids at The Outward Bound Trust and what a hell of a week it was!

To start it is a good four hour run blasting through some of the best roads North Wales could throw up and offer so I arrived with a grin on my face. That was soon wiped off when along with the other mentors we were taken around and asked to take part in a couple of the activities the kids would be aske to do during the week. No problem eh I am a grown man so what could they ask me to do that would be scary if they expected teenagers to so it.

They threw up a 30 foot high telegraph pole that you were to climb then stand on top of. Not too bad you are thinking right? Wrong. A 30 foot telegraph pole sways and wobbles when you are stood on top of it shaking so badly you look like you are dancing to techno music. Still once there the worse thing to do would be to come back down...the only way you are going to be doing that is by jumping from your perch to grab onto the trapeze swing dangling a few feet away at the same height as you.

That was my first change of pants.

All you had to do then while dangling on your swing was to trust your new found friends had tied the rope knots right and let go of the only thing you had hold off with a grip like death itself. Once swinging I have to say the view was pretty impressive though because until that point you had seen nothing but the red of terror in your eyes!

The kids had to do this...and they did it better than me!

160 teenagers turned up in a manic 20 minute window who were then told to get changed and do a "jog & Dip". Whenever I say "the kids" this ALWAYS includes me...I had to do everything they did. Well I didn't "have to" but it was expected and there was no way I was letting a bunch of hormone addled spotty kids think I was scared....I was crapping myself at times.

Anyway the jog & dip was a short half mile run, the last time I ran anywhere was with a large Doberman hard at my heels, to the sea where we promptly stood in a circle with our group of ten and dipped ourselves under the sea...cold does not even begin to express what the temperature was like! Sill the half mile jog back soon warmed us through along with more changing of pants.

Im not going to go into a detailed diary of the rest of the week because it would be a bit of a slog and I don't know if anyone else would be that interested but I will say the two day 11 mile hike up some of the biggest wind blown mountains North Wales had to offer along with wild camping saw the start of an incredible change in these teenagers. They started out as 10 awkward kids who didn't want to look at each other let alone talk to someone they didn't know god forbid that would happen but the hardships of hiking across difficult terrain, making camps as well as completing tasks as a team like when e dropped them onto a secluded beach with only the materials to make a raft so they could get back made a change in each and everyone of them that I would not have thought possible at the start of the week.

The kids grew up stopped thinking selfishly and considered their teammates. They supported, laughed and considered others but themselves. They pushed past mental limits protected and cared. They left at the end of the week different people with hope and determination that would put most adults to shame.

I was privileged to witness this. It was an incredible journey to be a part of and humbling to see.

Thanks to each and every one of you who donated toward this the charity know what they are doing this was not a holiday for these kids much to some surprise on their part but a life changing experience ad any advantage that can be given to those that need it is a good thing.
Land rover project updates will be back from tomorrow.

easye1   19th-October-2014 14:45

Re: The project has landed!

Quote:

The Outward Bound Trust
Brilliant report min....
be proud mate..

min200

Re: The project has landed!

Thanks chap it was an amazing experience. I learnt as much as the kids!
Thanks again to everyone who donated :)

min200

Re: The project has landed!

Filling up.
Main
Posted by min200 Mon, October 20, 2014 16:45:58

Wifey at work the kids at school and yet another cheeky day off at home for me so after the chaos of the past few weeks I actually got to don my babygrow and get near the landy.

My aim for the day was to get the fuel filler cap installed in place so I can actually put petrol in from the outside of the motor! I have been pestering folk for measurements of where their filler cap holes were (I originally typed "where their holes are" but after reading it back thought best to change it to spare myself some ridicule!) so when I chopped into the side of my landy the filler cap would be in the right place without a massive hole poking out from the edges... lets face it a big hole can spoil anyone's day.

The tape measure went out and in up and down until I was satisfied I had got it in the right place then came out the drill.
I thought it was best to start out with a small hole and work my way up from there until I got the dimensions just tight...I mean right!

The first hole was a bit tight...But I managed to stretch it out so I could get the sides of the framework in.
Once a snug fit was achieved I riveted it into place and fitted the main and overspill pipework in place. A quick couple of coats of paintwork later I managed to get the cap in and I have to say the results are quite impressive!

The only extra thing I had to get was an extra jubilee clip to keep the pipework in place next to the tank.

It looks like it was supposed to be in there all along now.

Another job ticked off of the list along with a bit of a wink toward this

elan23

Re: The project has landed!

Don't know what state the old tanks are in but if they are half decent get them on e-bay, they go for a bl**dy fortune. (change-over taps as well).

Damn, just read back and you've done that!

min200

Re: The project has landed!

Quote:

> Originally Posted by elan23 (Post 3253852)
> *Don't know what state the old tanks are in but if they are half decent get them on e-bay, they go for a bl**dy fortune. (change-over taps as well).*
>
> *Damn, just read back and you've done that!*

lol they did indeed go for a fortune and paid for my new wheels :)

TehNellie

The project has landed!

Don't have anything constructive to add to thread but did just want to say how much I've enjoyed reading it both for the landy updates and your "side project" with the kids.

I can't wait to see her finished:)

russ.star   22nd-October-2014 12:05

Re: The project has landed!

You need your own TV show .
Great write up

min200   22nd-October-2014 13:52

Re: The project has landed!

Thanks folks Im glad I am making a few folk smile :)

min200   22nd-October-2014 13:56

Re: The project has landed!

One down three to go.
Main
Posted by min200 Wed, October 22, 2014 13:50:38

Time to make a start on the brakes I just couldn't put it off any longer.
Brakes are not my favourite job on any project because its the one thing that always seems to throw up more issues and problems than I want or expect.

So I dug out the drum rebuild kits and decided on the off side rear drum would be my first victim. No reason why just looked like a good place start.
Wheel off drum off ok and the old rusty brake inners came into the light to say hello.
The rusty springs and old pads didn't take much getting off.
Now the brake pipes were another matter! You know I said something ALWAYS goes wrong well the pipe nut on the back of the cylinder rounded off on the first turn.

The metal had gone soft which is a shame because I thought the pipes would be ok and not need replacing but after a good luck and scrape it turns out about half of them are past their best. Hey ho I have learnt not to panic over such things and just get on with sorting them now but I will replace all of the pipework from front to back.

I had to undo the brake pipe at the union on the axle taking off the extra fittings to slide out the cylinder.

The new brake pads and cylinder were duly dropped in. Sounds easy eh? was it buggery! The hooks on the springs were too long but a quick grind got them o the right length and made fitting them a bit easier. I fitted the base spring first because well they are awkward fitting from behind the pads when they are on the drums.

One corner done and only three more to go. I bloody hate brakes.

easye1
22nd-October-2014 20:01

Re: The project has landed!

lol..
agree brakes are a pain, but more pain without them..
Q. 1... are you using a brake pipe nut spanner - its like a ring spanner but thicker (tougher) but has a slit to go over the pipe then onto the blinkin nut....
its just a hexagon so has less chance of rounding off.
Q no. 2...if the brake pipes are a total loss, you can cut them off at the top of the nut and use a "good" fitting hex socket to undo them with.......even if you find a slightly smaller hex socket a tap it on with a hammer GENTLY it will make undoing easier ;)

or am I teaching grandma to suck eggs....lol

min200
22nd-October-2014 23:29

Re: The project has landed!

Cutting them off at the top of the nut was the way forward ;)

I mean why struggle with trying to get the bloody thing out of a part you are about to throw away anyway!??

Never too old or experienced to learn something new fella...Im definitely getting old and still stupid enough to have a go at most things the hard way round!

easye1

Re: The project has landed!

Quote:

> Originally Posted by min200 (Post 3256853)
> *Cutting them off at the top of the nut was the way forward ;)*
>
> *I mean why struggle with trying to get the bloody thing out of a part you are about to throw away anyway!??*
>
> *Never too old or experienced to learn something new fella...Im definitely getting old and still stupid enough to have a go at most things the hard way round!*

nice to know chap..;)

min200

Re: The project has landed!

Pounds & Pennies
Main
Posted by min200 Thu, October 23, 2014 08:35:49

Does anyone else get messed around at work? I seem to have a face that attracts it, maybe because I am an easy going guy but maybe they just like to take the piss and are waiting to see how long it will be before I loose the plot and start killing folks there who knows.

I have gone from a start time in the afternoon to a morning start time again after being informed "due to a reshuffle your start time doesn't exist anymore" I mean don't they realise what this means? I will have to come home in the early evening just like a normal person and see the Wife and kids SEVEN DAYS A WEEK!!! My god the secret to a happy marriage has been only saving that horror for the weekends before so now I will have to listen to the drivel that teenage girls and wives spout on a daily basis! Still could be worse I suppose...I don't know how yet but I will find something to take solace in as the day goes by.

Time to update the Landy Project costs as its been a while. All receipts were put in a pile so I wouldn't lose track and I finally got around to totting up what I had sold off of the project and for how much.

I want the costing list to be a true projection of how much money I have into it. What I mean to say is how much of my hard earned cash out of my own pocket so I seeing as I have put back into every penny the project has generated I have classed this as a credit because I didn't have to earn it (apart from putting a few adverts up but that doesn't class as work in my book).

The amazing thing is the Landy has given me more money back than I paid for it to start with and I have the thing sat on my driveway! I know that's a rare occurrence these days but its also left me feeling a bit smug!

So all in all the project costs are still looking good and my aim now is to get it roadworthy by the end of January, it was Christmas but with my new start time at work I don't think that's going to be possible.

Landy Project Costs

Land Rover £375

Sanding Discs £11.70

Ignition Barrel £20

Heritage letter £21.75

2x Batteries and rear 1/4 light £35

Pair Battery Terminal Clamps £3.99

Floor pan nuts & bolts £6.50

Grinding disc £2.25

Under Seal £8.99

Complete set of lights £85

5 Litres Primer £24.99

4 Discovery Wheels £10.20

Rear Door £21.00

Front Door £20.00

Handbrake spring £1.50

2 Discovery wheels

Two seatbelts

Wing Mirror

2 Headlight surrounds

2 headlight frames £60

2 Front Doors £60

Nato Green Paint £36

Rear Window Seal and insert £9.99

Wiring connectors £3.00

2 tins of silver metal paint £7.00

Fuses & Sandpaper £4.50

5x tins black spray £5.00

5x more tins black spray £5.00

Clutch fluid

Exhaust putty

WD40 £8.49

Car Boot Bits £13

Front & rear shocks £59.45

Front & rear brake rebuild kits £81.62

Fuel tank & filler £40

Wheels complete with tyres £250

Fuel pump

Fuel hose

Indicator stalk

Bonnet strap

Brake switch

Fuel pump gasket

Fuel line clips £67.74

24v Wiper motor

24v flasher relay

24v heater

24v front loom

oil cooler

Door tops x2

Rear bench seat £67.50

Roof rack £100

Wheel nuts £8

Brake pipe kit £39

Wheels £250

CREDIT FOR BITS SOLD OFF OF PROJECT £389

TOTAL £1388.16

russ.star

Re: The project has landed!

[quote=min200;3256904]Pounds & Pennies
Main
Posted by min200 Thu, October 23, 2014 08:35:49

Does anyone else get messed around at work? I seem to have a face that attracts it, maybe because I am an easy going guy but maybe they just like to take the piss and are waiting to see how long it will be before I loose the plot and start killing folks there who knows.

I have gone from a start time in the afternoon to a morning start time again after being informed "due to a reshuffle your start time doesn't exist anymore" I mean don't they realise what this means? **I will have to come home in the early evening just like a normal person and see the Wife and kids SEVEN DAYS A WEEK!!! My god the secret to a happy marriage has been only saving that horror for the weekends before so now I will have to listen to the drivel that teenage girls and wives spout on a daily basis!** Still could be worse I suppose...I don't know how yet but I will find something to take solace in as the day goes by.

hysterically_laughing!!!!

Brown

Re: The project has landed!

[quote=russ.star;3257009]
   Quote:

     Originally Posted by min200 (Post 3256904)
     Pounds & Pennies
     Main
     Posted by min200 Thu, October 23, 2014 08:35:49

     Does anyone else get messed around at work? I seem to have a fa

     I have gone from a start time in the afternoon to a morning start t

     :hysterically_laughi

Well, isn't that what Land Rovers are for? That and a shed.

min200

23rd-October-2014 20:56

Re: The project has landed!

Indeed they are ;)

Brown

Re: The project has landed!

When I'm busy with a big job like a brake rebuild or a suspension rebuild my partner describes herself as a 'Land Rover widow'.

min200

Re: The project has landed!

Quote:

Originally Posted by Brown (Post 3258922)
When I'm busy with a big job like a brake rebuild or a suspension rebuild my partner describes herself as a 'Land Rover widow'.

:D:D:D When the Landy magazines arrive Wife shouts "Your Porn is here!"

Re: The project has landed!

Padded Corners
Main
Posted by min200 Sat, October 25, 2014 18:02:46

I had bought tickets to go to a Medieval Fair at Nottingham Castle today for me and my youngest as Wifey was off first thing to a Spa for a fiends birthday. Well my daughter dumped me at the first chance to go away on holiday for a week with my parents I mean who would rather go away with their grandparents to be spoilt rotten for a week when you could go for a few hours to look at folk dressed up like jesters and the like eh?

I'm glad she went because the Fair was bloody awful. Don't get me wrong here there was a lot of effort put into by the "players" and if you were seven or under it would have been a spellbinding place I am sure but as an adult it was, lets say, cringe worthy. Each to their own.

Luckily the castle, which is well worth a visit at any time you are passing, was holding a large display in the gallery about The Great War and its effects on the local folk who both fought in it and those lefty behind here. I am just going to take a moment here and say we owe so very much to those lads that fought and died in the most awful of surrounds. We owe al of our forces both now and then our way of life and our luxuries thank you just doesn't seem enough does it?

After a couple of hours milling about I forced a KFC down my neck for lunch (be rude not to while in town) ad headed home to see if I could finish those pads off on the last three corners. I have to look at brakes that way "the last three" because I do hate doing the spiteful bloody things.

I went for a change in tactics today because I knew the clocks are going back tonight so not as much light later in the day to play and the fact Wifey will be back around lunchtime to spoil/tell me about her pampering stuff. It will have something to do with hot stones and massage I am sure but what I am not so sure about is that it all sounds like a list of what's available at the local whore house.

So first I finished off the back brakes and this all went rather swimmingly. I plugged myself into my music, this is a first for me whilst working on the landy but I fancied a change, and set to removing the front wheel and old brakes along with the cylinders. An elderly gentleman walked past looking me directly in the face and grinning wildly which seems a bit odd but we live in a city and there are a few odd balls about.

The front brakes have the twin cylinders so this made the job of refitting the pads a lot easier as you only have to battle on spring at a time instead of the two on the back end. Time for a change of album on the phone and the wheel went back on.

A couple of spotty teenagers walked past staring at me and grinning away...again bloody odd twice in a row but maybe they think I look daft in my bandana you know with me being over twenty one and all.

The last corner beckoned so I delved in full of confidence at how easy this was going to be because I had worked out a couple of tricks on how to slide the pads in using a large screwdriver. New album and a bit of country music this time always good for making you feel happy. So moving my head in time to the music I notice a mum and her kids walking past me staring away and smiling like Cheshire cats so this is getting creepy now. I have been working on the Landy how long? and no one has ever walked past staring away at me and looking at me like I am the funniest looking ape in the zoo so surely there must be something daft on my face? A quick check in the door mirror proves nothings wrong just a devilishly handsome chap staring back so the last brakes get my attention again.

The new cylinders fitted, on auto pilot because I'm good at this now, but something looked amiss...
Yep fitted the bloody things backwards. Not just the top mind when I should have noticed it but the bottom as well! The suns out and the country mix has me tapping away so no bother just undo all the nuts and change them around again.
Chucked the new pads on and it looked much better.

Tidy up time and a lad in his mid twenties walks past mostly looking down with a smirk on his face and the odd furtive glance my way and I have to say people are starting to piss me off now because not only are they rude but the next who smirks or grins at me like a nut job is going to get a serious amount of abuse.

I throw my tools in the back of the Landy and spend ten minutes just taping up a few wires and fitting an inline fuel filter. Then As I walk up the side of my house my neighbour is stood there smiling like a nut job at me so enough is enough and I pull out my head phones and say to him "Why are you smiling at me like you havejust taken all the bloody happy pills? Loads of people have been all day and its starting to piss me right off" to which he replies without missing a beat...

"It's your singing voice chap, very dulcet tone indeed and an all afternoon performance for free!"

Apparently he is going to copy me in on the videos of it going up on you tube.

easye1   25th-October-2014 23:32

Re: The project has landed!

:lol:

but then, you was happy eh.....

my 14yo grandaughter is just the same when she stays with us, pinches my big `ol cans if shes forgot her dr beats or whatever, but the off key droning goes on for ages...

anyway, a man who never made a mistake is a man who`s done nothing
(with landrovers).....lol

I refuse to speak of your calling brake linings "pads" - so there.. :)

min200   26th-October-2014 08:06

Re: The project has landed!

They are bloody pads...the linings are the bit stuck on the metal ;)

It has been suggested I enter the X factor....more for the idiots at the start that make arses out of themselves im sure!

min200   26th-October-2014 12:29

Re: The project has landed!

The strangest memory popped into my head this morning t was one of those things you notice when you are out and about think to yourself "that's a bit odd" but carry on with whatever task you were doing at the time.

It was at work on Wednesday evening and the heavens had opened up. The rain was coming down sideways and I was dropping a trailer onto a bay when I say a driver come out of the building covering his BALD head with a bit of A4 paper while running toward his truck. What's odd about that you ask? well break it down.

He was trying to protect his head with an A4 sized bit of paper now lets face it you are not going to be covering up much with that are you?

Oh and he was as BALD as a baby's backside. He could have casually strolled through a waterfall and only would have had to wipe his hand over his shiny dome to dry it!

Maybe it was some built in primal instinct to cover his full and funky locks from days gone by who knows.

OK then My project is coming along nicely so it was time to look at the electrics and here is what we have going on.

The Front headlights and side lights work just fine.

The indicators only work on the off side.

The hazards only work on the offside.

The rear side lights only work on the offside.

Fog lights don't work at all.

The horn, wipers and washers don't work.

have taken the dash off and there is this wire just floating about looking like it should be attached somewhere...
It's the small wire at the right hand side of the dials.

The fuse box looks past its best if I am honest with corrosion on the terminals and if you move it around the dash instruments work then don't then do!
The pile of freshly cooked spaghetti behind the dash looks like its going to be great fun! I am learning as I go here on the electrical front on Land rovers and its looking like it will be a steep curve!

I have pleaded for help across a few forums so I will update as and when I make any sort of headway.

As for those of you who re thinking to themselves "hang on I thought he was doing the brakes?" you are right and yes I am but I'm a bit stuck until the new pipework arrives next week so I thought I would give myself a stroke by pretending to be a sparky for the morning!

3.5 efi

26th-October-2014 12:33

Re: The project has landed!

Would guess thats come from the screw terminal.

easye1

26th-October-2014 12:51

Re: The project has landed!

unless you already have a better one, a cheap and cheerful electrical

tester is a godsend.
you can check each wire for power before guessing its home.
also as usefull is a length of circuit wire with a crocodile clip on one end, a perhaps pointy bit on the other with an inline fuse near to the end you hold.
connect the crocodile clip to power source = battery
and use the mobile power lead to "touch" electrical circuits at bulb holders and such that dont work to see if they do work when powered up - even if it momenterily so ...
it defines whether the bulb/bulbholder is no good, or the supply is no good.

being old school I always carry a length of wire under the discos bonnet but as said length of wire but with crocodile clips at each end. if I loose power while out somewhere, one end clips on to battery power, the other clips to lost power source to light an unlit bulb.....till I can get home and sort it propperly in the daylight.

it has other uses I will not repeat on here ;)

min200

26th-October-2014 12:59

Re: The project has landed!

Sounds like a plan chap. Be getting myself some clips and wire then ;)

Bought myself a cheap tester a few months back...still learning how to use the damn thing properly!

easye1   26th-October-2014 13:13

Re: The project has landed!

Quote:

> Originally Posted by min200 (Post 3260197)
> *Sounds like a plan chap. Be getting myself some clips and wire then ;)*
>
> *Bought myself a cheap tester a few months back...still learning how to use the damn thing properly!*

cheap testers are great, I only used the DC section, adjusted to the power range that needs testing = 24volts in your case ??

If like mine its powered by a 9volt battery, ensure its switch to off before you put away....

(I have a few spare 9volt batteries coz = :o..)

min200   26th-October-2014 14:50

Re: The project has landed!

Yep 24 volts for me! Getting there with it now...I think lol

Re: The project has landed!

Lights on.
Main
Posted by min200 Sun, November 02, 2014 17:01:13

I've been looking forward to today all week. It was the one morning that I had nothing booked in and no chores to run so it was to be time to put the brakes back together.

I woke up to the sound of pouring rain hitting the bedroom window so plans had o change. I admit I was feeling a bit peeved to say the least as the prospect of getting over another milestone on the old project was appealing but seeing as I have no garage to work in I am at the mercy of mother nature and as much as I would like to make her do differently she is a fickle mistress who will do as she pleases.

The ran passed by nine thirty but the driveway was soaked so no lying on it for today but I then remembered I had a load of electrical bits to be sorting out on it as seeing as most of that is inside I grabbed my babygrow and hopped in.

After looking at the fuse box last week I ordered a new one because the corrosion was pretty bad on the contacts.
It didn't look any better when I had taken all of the wiring off so I think I made the right call here!
Obviously I have taken pictures to make sure I put the wiring back in the right place and not cause myself any unnecessary headaches but the shiny new one looked good before putting it on.

All surprisingly went well and with everything refitted I had a check through to see if it had cured any issues at all...it had! The wipers now work and I am hoping the washers will too once they are refitted as its the same button (I think but im probably wrong!) To say such a simple noise form a motor and a simple action such as the rotten old wipers smearing themselves across the screen can bring such a feeling of happiness is very very true....it felt like Christmas and I felt like a proper mechanic right up until I checked out the indicators on the near side. They still were not working.

SO I set to work changing over the indicator relay that had turned up in a box of bits that I bought a few weeks back and had been living down south in my Dads shed until I collected them yesterday. It made no difference at all the light sat there doing nothing and taunting me silently..."I am no mechanic" I thought as the euphoria of getting the wipers working faded away.
Out came the trusty multimeter I bought some time back and with apprehension I tested the bulb holder wiring both front and back. There was power to the back one so I checked it over cleaned it up and put the bulb back in place...let there be light!

One down and one to go....the front one didn't want to play but I managed to figure out there was power up until where the wires joined for the holder but none after it. Connections checked and still nothing happening so I delved into my box of spares and pulled out a spare bulb holder wired it up and it worked!!!!!!!!! Drilling out the rivets holding on the old one was a quick and easy affair along with fitting the replacement. Indication is no longer a problem for me nor is the hazard warning for the many times I will undoubtedly be broken down on the roadside!

The fog lights just will not play though. I only get a faint reading of power anywhere on the circuit so that will be solved either by the excellent advice I get on the forums or by removing the lights and switch altogether as they are not a legal requirement on a 1983 motor.

I cant find the horn either? It was getting dark but im buggered if I can see it??? Still another job for another day. All in all a good day in dragging my Landy back to life!

easye1

Re: The project has landed!

great work....

min200

Re: The project has landed!

Alcohol.

Main
Posted by min200 Sun, November 09, 2014 08:31:31

I have changed...long gone are the days of boozing heavily getting up and starting again the next lunchtime. Last night I had 3 pints of Hobgoblin a bottle of Budweiser and a shot of something green. I am glad I stopped there because my backside stinks worse than a rotting dog and this morning I am teetering on the edge of having a hangover and that's enough of a reminder that I don't like them very much. Also what is with not being able to sleep properly when you have had more than a couple of drinks? Is it just me or does everyone else have this happen as well? I am a grown up now or just a proper lightweight?

I will stick to my bottle of beer and cheeky vodka on a weekend evening from now on but the reason for a few extra's was it was the mother in laws surprise 60th Birthday party. It was that much of a surprise I didnt know about it until yesterday morning but according to the Wifey she told me weeks ago. The reasons I was a bit miffed about it were the fact I didnt want to go and we were supposed to be off out with the Nottingham Land Rover Club for a bonfire and play away off road...bloody family lol.

Today is a free pass day though so I get to go and try to finish my brakes off but I wanted to do a quick update on parts bought and sold. I managed to sell the two way tank switch for a nice sum and I bought a new exhaust system, flexi hose pipes and a proper number plate light. Below are the latest figures and I will update later about how many brake pipes I ruined changing them over later!

Landy Project Costs

Land Rover £375

Sanding Discs £11.70

Ignition Barrel £20

Heritage letter £21.75

2x Batteries and rear 1/4 light £35

Pair Battery Terminal Clamps £3.99

Floor pan nuts & bolts £6.50

Grinding disc £2.25

Under Seal £8.99

Complete set of lights £85

5 Litres Primer £24.99

4 Discovery Wheels £10.20

Rear Door £21.00

Front Door £20.00

Handbrake spring £1.50

2 Discovery wheels

Two seatbelts

Wing Mirror

2 Headlight surrounds

2 headlight frames £60

2 Front Doors £60

Nato Green Paint £36

Rear Window Seal and insert £9.99

Wiring connectors £3.00

2 tins of silver metal paint £7.00

Fuses & Sandpaper £4.50

5x tins black spray £5.00

5x more tins black spray £5.00

Clutch fluid

Exhaust putty

WD40 £8.49

Car Boot Bits £13

Front & rear shocks £59.45

Front & rear brake rebuild kits £81.62

Fuel tank & filler £40

Wheels complete with tyres £250

Fuel pump

Fuel hose

Indicator stalk

Bonnet strap

Brake switch

Fuel pump gasket

Fuel line clips £67.74

24v Wiper motor

24v flasher relay

24v heater

24v front loom

oil cooler

Door tops x2

Rear bench seat £67.50

Roof rack £100

Wheel nuts £8

Brake pipe kit £39

Wheels & Tyres £250

Exhaust System & Flexi hose pipes £66

Number plate light £5

CREDIT FOR BITS SOLD OFF OF PROJECT £424

TOTAL £1414.16

payydg

Re: The project has landed!

Quote:

I feel your pain. Alcohol is an anaesthetic and like all aesthetics it stops you going into REM sleep. Cycling between different sleep cycles (esp REM) is whats needed for high quality, refreshing sleep. Which is why you feel knackered no matter how many hours of 'unconciousness' you've had.

min200
9th-November-2014 17:40

Re: The project has landed!

Thank God I am not a big boozer! I dont sleep much anyway so sleep lost has a big effect!
Not boozing saves a fortune as well we spent £50 last night and have bugger all to show for it! Could have gone towards some seat lol

min200
9th-November-2014 19:36

Re: The project has landed!

Brake pipes

Main
Posted by min200 Sun, November 09, 2014 19:31:57

Well that was shits and giggles from the start. "Change the brake pipes" I thought "how hard can it be" I thought "I mean its only nuts on the end of pipe so should be done in a couple of hours."

Try all bloody day from breakfast until the light went out of the sky. I bought a kit because I am lazy and it would save cutting and flaring the pipe but I am so very glad I did because if it took me all day to fit the ready made stuff I would have been there a week building the pipes as well.

It started ok with the rear pipes coming off easily enough and the new pipe going on. It was at this early stage though that I realised that each of the pipes had been cut a little bit longer than was needed and this would prove a pain later on the longer bits when I had to be inventive in bending it in such a way that I could lose some of the length into gaps where it wouldnt get ripped off when I am off road.
So the back done and the long pipe from front to back bent into places I tackled the front brakes. The flexi hose were shot so I decided they had to be replaced.
Came off easy enough.
The new hose went on no problem along with the new pipe from hose to drums but when I came to fitting the link pipe from the top of the drum to the bottom I realised I had made a mistake...it is almost impossible to fit the bottom of the link pipe to the bottom brake calliper with the calliper fitted to the back plate.
Off came the newly fitted pads and then the calliper removed so I could feed the pipe through the back plate screw it in place then refit all snug and tidy.

The only other issue I had was the master brake cylinder. This must either be an odd military spec one or the pipe kit had the wrong screw fitting on one pipe end because the screw/nut that goes into my master cylinder closest to the front of the motor is a larger size. Seems a bit odd but hey what do I know and luckily these front two pipes were the only ones that were any good so I took them off and gave them a clean up before refitting. Of course one of the screw ends did not want to go back where it had come from for a good twenty minutes but two skinned knuckles and a few new kick dents in place all is well.

I have this old oil can type of drip tray...
Now this is a fantastic bit of kit for when you are draining oils out of anything and for any leaks you have going on and this one was doing just this when I backed up under the Landy bending pipework into place whilst simultaneously dipping th eback of my skull into it. With an oily skull I jerked upwards into the chassis with my forehead then back down hard into the concrete driveway with my wet skull both cracking it hard and collecting plenty of rusty dust and general dirt.

I love rebuilding my Landy at times and at other times I wonder what the hell I have started....

easye1   9th-November-2014 20:49

Re: The project has landed!

LOL..
"I love rebuilding my Landy at times and at other times I wonder what the hell I have started"

think most owners of older landies feel the same at times,
but for me, it`s when I climb into mine, get comfy, turn that key to start, and as it idles while I get my seat belt on, phone charger connected, first gear - handbrake of,
I`m already smiling again....

min200   9th-November-2014 21:42

Re: The project has landed!

Quote:

One day my friend one day.......;)

Jacobjm

10th-November-2014 13:16

Re: The project has landed!

That is one of a classic masterpiece.

min200

10th-November-2014 23:31

Re: The project has landed!

Quote:

:D:D:D:D Thanks fella! :)

min200

Re: The project has landed!

Bleeding Brakes.

Main
Posted by min200 Mon, November 10, 2014 23:29:47

This is always a fun job trying to force the air out of a new brake system and get the nice new brake fluid through the shiny pipes so I have treated myself to a shiny new tool that I have been told will solve all of my problems from the above and quickly to boot!

I bought a new toy a brake vacuum bleeding kit.
So any ideas on how it works? No? Me neither could I find the instructions?? Nope that was nicely tucked away so you couldnt see it in that slot so I did my best impression of a monkey on the Krypton Factor trying to solve the winning puzzle before I knocked the whole case off of its perch on top of the motorbike scattering the whole bloody lot across the drive and the instructions took on a new lease of life at being freed making a gentle fluttering dash into the dual carriageway that runs past my front door. Once I picked up the mess up the manual was very helpful!

Once I had the kit put together I remembered to take the top off of the fluid reservoir which is most helpful as is putting the fluid in the system! You work the vacuum pump in order of nearest to the servo first then working away from it. The first three corners went well enough, apart from a small puddle of fluid on the front nearside wheel where I had forgotten to tighten the pipe nut up then had me crawling around checking them all convinced I must be getting early onset dementia, and left me thinking what a good investment I had made but would the last and furthest corner bleed through??? No it would not.

After an hour of more right hand action than my wrist has seen in years I threw in the towel and dug out my old bleeding pipe with the non return valve on the end and the last stubborn corner was finished air free with a firm brake pedal and a huge smile on my face!

The brake pads were then adjusted up properly and I went and grabbed some lunch. As the day was going so well and I had a couple of hours to kill before having to meet one of the many daughters for an evening meal I thought I would whip off the old rotten exhaust. This too went really well with old rusty nuts giving in to my spanners at the first hurdle and the three nuts on the exhaust manifold played as well! What a day I was having this really is superb!

The rear and mid sections fell off no worries that just left the front section. This is still stuck under the bloody car. Can I get the damned thing out? Nope its still out there laughing at me. I need to jack the front of the motor up a lot more to get the damned thing out and the new section in, oh that and an angle grinder. Im chopping the old one out first because it has a bad attitude has been laughing at me and just needs teaching a lesson, by "teaching a lesson" I mean I am going to kick its head in cut it into small pieces and bury it on the allotments out back.

Brown   11th-November-2014 09:09

Re: The project has landed!

Yes, there's a lot of air can hide in a Land Rover braking system and it takes quite a while to bleed it all through, particularly on the passenger side rear. You might want to let it settle overnight and bleed it some more the following day and you'll get even more bubbles out. I got one of those things that pressurizes the master cylinder and it still takes me ages.

min200   11th-November-2014 15:36

Re: The project has landed!

My thoughts as well on the bleed it again front! Bought some more fluid yesterday but couldn't face them again today after two days straight on the bloody things lol maybe at the weekend again!

min200   11th-November-2014 16:08

Re: The project has landed!

Showers of sparks

Main
Posted by min200 Tue, November 11, 2014 16:02:50

There were chores to do. I couldn't put them off any longer. The dog was following me around like a lost puppy wanting a walk the warm autumn still had the grass growing so I had to coax one last cut out of the old knackered mower that the wheels keep falling off and last but not least the driveway had all of the leaves from every tree in the neighbourhood piled high in the corners.

On the plus side it didn't take too long to get sorted and then the fun commenced! I dug out the grinder and went smirking to myself to the stuck exhaust piece..
What a shame I was finally going to get to kill it!
It took all of 30 seconds to cut it away and we were then in business!
The reason for fitting a new exhaust isnt because the old one looked rusty it was solid enough but the problem was this....

It was a bit flat to say the least and it wasn't letting a great deal of exhaust gas through. Out with the old and in with the new. I jacked up the front of the Landy another notch on the axle stands which gave me enough clearance to fit the new front pipe without a repeat of getting stuck again. The whole system fitted in no problem along with new brackets and bolts.

All shiny and new!!!! It wont take long to cure that problem.
With that done quicker than expected and while the grinder was out I went to work on removing the last of the FFR brackets out of the rear tub. I had to move a couple of boxes around and somehow managed to set off the fire extinguisher with one...
At least I know it would have worked if I had needed it!
I attacked the FFR brackets with the grinder and gusto then soon enough they were all out as well.
Onto Ebay they will go! Every penny helps towards the rebuild. Then seeing as I had nothing better to do I fitted the rear seat I had picked up. That was an easy job just two holes to drill and hey presto all sorted.
It's been a good few days off of work and I feel like I have now come over the hill top with this project. With any luck it will be on the road soon and then I will have to choose another project to be getting on with! Maybe a Discovery next time....

Re: The project has landed!

Not a lot doing.

Main
Posted by min200 Sun, November 16, 2014 16:21:06

Autumn weather sucks. Its bloody dark early and cold normally wet
then nonsense like Christmas shopping turns up out of the blue that
I get dragged along to God knows why its not like I get to give any
input into the choice of anything at all. Well that last bit is not strictly
true I get to give my input which duly gets a nod from Wifey who
then tells me I am wrong and does what she wants anyway.
So I managed to grab an hour earlier to have a go on the Landy. I
thought I would get the old girl started so put in some fuel and bled
it through. Turned the key to find out that the batteries are about flat
so no turnover there. I mean endless hours of having the lights on
sorting the electrics shouldn't flatten two old batteries that havn't
been charged in three months should it eh! Ok I know I was lucky to
have them last that long but dumb ass that I ma should have put
them on charge yesterday but hey ho if that was going to be the
worse thing that happened today then it will still be a good day.

The replacement fuel tank leaks.

I'm hoping its because the seal has been dry for some time and it
will swell up again but I suppose I will find out tomorrow. If it needs
a new fuel tank then so be it we are that far in now it doesn't really
matter.
I then jumped underneath the Landy and spray painted the prop
shafts and axles black to tidy them up. Forgot to take pictures of that

and I wasn't getting back under it in the wet to do it so that can be saved for a future post.
Then I changed the back wheels over to the new ones that are going on and removed the axle stands...must be getting somewhere a set of axle stands is away!
I have been meaning to buy black paint for the front window frame for months and today forgot it yesterday so seeing as there was no rain I painted the bugger green for now.
While the paint was out I gave the battery cover box a once over as well.
Then it was time to go out with the youngest daughter to buy something she "desperately" needed. Luckily I looked in the mirror before I left....
Paint on the nose...without noticing....I mean how???

easye1

Re: The project has landed!

Quote:

"Paint on the nose...without noticing....I mean how???"

ever seen the statue - "the thinker" - think its called..
sitting, hand on head,
or in your case hand on nose perhaps....
Oh, the landie -- Its looking cracking mate....or good job as the yanks, or my 5yo grandson would say - hees an essex boy also, so cant explain that either :confused:

Re: The project has landed!

Ticking over

Main
Posted by min200 Mon, November 17, 2014 12:09:49

Last night I charged up the batteries so this morning I could get the engine running again.
I popped both of them into place wired them up and turned the ignition over but it wouldnt start! I figured I hadnt yet pulled enough fuel through the new pump and pipework so pumped away again to my hearts content for a couple of minutes. It's bloody awkward reaching that pump handle you have to bend over and practically lie on the engine top to do it...well a short arse like me does.
That was enough to fire her up and I was happy to hear the exhaust system was sealed and the dash dials were working nicely. I watched as all the old dust and dirt in those hard to get places burnt away and the temperature needle started to climb.
I forgot to say yesterday that I tested the brakes out with the help of my youngest again and they all worked! I had to tweak a couple but all is well there now so that pleased me no end!
Back to the engine though the temperature had hit the middle of the dial so I thought it best to check that the thermostat was working seeing as it has been in there for so long. I reached for the pipe running from the top of the housing to the radiator and this is where It got Interesting.
You know those big metal fan blades that help cool your rad the ones that are normally painted blue...mine are red now.

The Landy demanded a larger blood offering this time before I am allowed to finish it completely well that's what I am going with

anyway because it sounds better than "I am a dozy pillock that shouldn't be allowed near moving engine parts".
I felt for the top pipe to check for heat slipped and pushed my fingers into the rotating metal fan blades.

To say I have been lucky is an understatement. My first finger went in and got skinned on the side and split next to the side of the nail, my third finger came worse off with a blade going in and out just below the finger nail on the tip very deeply but coming out again before it took the whole tip with it! All fingers are nicely bruised and bloody painful but hey it could have been so very much worse.
Now we all hurt ourselves often when playing around with motors and normally just shrug off the pain thinking "knobhead" and the like but you know that feeling when you KNOW you have done some real damage...I have not felt that in a long time and am in no rush to do it again. I have to take the week off of work, just what I need on the run up to Christmas, but at least its only a week. I can remove the Steri strips on Saturday after a good soaking but until then I am not allowed to get it wet, dirty or put any pressure on it at all. Doesn't it seem like a lot of fuss for a cut lol
The nurse seemed to take sadistic pleasure in cleaning it out that smarted a bit!
A week to kill and nothing to do because if I touch The Landy Wifey will kill me. I cannot write a great deal because dong it left handed is an interesting experience and this blog entry has taken me an hour...best get some books out of the library!

min200

17th-November-2014 12:13

Re: The project has landed!

Quote:

The thinker..me?..nah lol You want to hear the nonsense my kids come out with! I often ask them "When did we move to America then?"

min200   17th-November-2014 19:47

Westwood8055   18th-November-2014 14:13

The project has landed!

Just read all of this thread, great work and very well written, subscribed and looking forward to future posts.

min200

Re: The project has landed!

Quote:

> Originally Posted by Westwood8055 (Post 3284369)
> *Just read all of this thread, great work and very well written, subscribed and looking forward to future posts.*

Thanks :) that is much appreciated! I do enjoy writing the posts as well, it calms me :crazy::D

min200

18th-November-2014 16:39

Re: The project has landed!

Caught red handed!

Main
Posted by min200 Tue, November 18, 2014 16:38:43

You know I am banned from doing anything on the Landy until the weekend at the soonest so my poor little fingers get a chance to heal a bit well Wifey was at work the kids at school/college and after somehow cleaning out the chicken coop and the Dragons vivarium one handed over a couple of hours I got to sit down with a cup of tea.
As I sat there looking out of the dining room window at the Land

Rover the devil inside started chipping away at me.

"Just have a look around it that will be ok"
"Might as well have a sit in it and smell that project oil"
"No one is in...no one will ever know"
"Its ok as long you don't do anything to it"
"You have your "good" clothes on so you wouldn't dare get them dirty!"

My resolve soon crumbled and I found myself sitting in the drivers seat with the keys in my hand, what harm could starting it do?

The key turned the engine coughed into life and I sat surrounded by the sweet burble of the 2 1/4 petrol engine ticking over. Seeing as it was running I decided to let it get really warmed up and watched the temp gauge rise steadily. Now there is another way of seeing if your thermostat works rather than shoving your fingers into the radiator blades and this is by watching your temperature gauge. It will climb and climb while you sit with the engine running then it will drop down a fair bit once the thermostat opens then steadily climb a bit until it finds it running level.
This is what I did. I sat there with my fingers throbbing with worry about a repeat of yesterdays performance in the warmth of the heater looking at the dash water and oil temp levels sitting nicely bang in the middle where they should be and the only fault I found with the arctic heater in that the air seems to be blowing out of the bottom of the unit rather than out of the pipework it was supposed to come from so no biggy just a bit of a fix. All is well my project is nearing completion.
This is when my eldest daughter walked up the drive. I didn't see her coming because I was sitting with my head back in the drivers seat just enjoying the engine noise...caught red handed.
She had that look on her face that daughters can only ever learn from their mothers, you know the one that look that you remember from childhood the on ewhere its a mixture of stern consternation and disapproval that you are doing exactly the thing you KNOW you

should not be doing...Busted!

"DAD YOU ARE NOT ALLOWED TO BE WORKING ON THAT WITH YOUR HAND YOU WILL MAKE YOURSELF WORSE!"

"How do I get out of this then?" I thought to myself. In a split second my mind ran through thousands of possibilities and settled on a winner. She's learning to drive you see...she is getting a bit of a thing for Land Rovers now and really quite fancies a SWB you see....she has never sat in one and really wants to drive one....I had to be subtle to pull this off.
"You are right kid you are right that's why I am just running the new exhaust in" (A vicious lie I know but she has no idea about mechanics so why not) "I have to do it before servicing the engine properly...fancy a sit in the drivers seat to help?"
The look in her eyes changed from suspicion to excitement as she jumped into the seat and revved the engine a few times. "Like it?" I asked. "Yea" she said with a massive grin on her face...I might just pull this off...
"Good kid its great eh! Look don't tell your Mother I was in it not that I was "working" on it just sitting there but she will just worry and I will let you drive it as soon as it has an MOT on it"
She looked at me sideways with a mix of knowing what I was doing and temptation...temptation won. She says it's a deal so I may dodge the wrath of Wifey on this one but if the daughter is anything like the mother it will cost me dearly!#

easye1

Re: The project has landed!

very thin ice lad, very thin ice indeed...........................lol

min200

Re: The project has landed!

Quote:

> Originally Posted by easye1 (Post 3284568)
> *very thin ice lad, very thin ice indeed...........................lol*

Seemed like a good idea at the time!

min200

Re: The project has landed!

Facebook page.

Main
Posted by min200 Tue, November 18, 2014 20:26:43

OK then folks my kids have told me I need a Facebook page for my blog as well as the site itself.

So the link is below and please join up folks and "Like" the page and "Share" it...well thats what I am told anyway!

https://www.facebook.com/groups/396056643881797/

Greenie85

Re: The project has landed!

Crikey that is a high risk strategy indeed!
On a different note this really is an excellent blog. I've greatly enjoyed reading this

min200

Re: The project has landed!

Quote:

> Originally Posted by Greenie85 (Post 3284910)
> *Crikey that is a high risk strategy indeed!*
> *On a different note this really is an excellent blog. I've greatly enjoyed reading this*

You are not wrong on the Facewipe stuff...havnt a bloody clue!
People are asking to be added and theres a long lost relative in

Zimbabwe who says I have loads of inheritance out there and all he needed was my bank details!

Seriously I am glad you are enjoying t my driffle because I do like writing it!

min200

Re: The project has landed!

Throbbing.

Main
Posted by min200 Wed, November 19, 2014 13:55:21

I awoke to just the one finger hurting the one with the big slice in so I thought to myself that it was a bonus the finger tip bruising is easing off. That lasted until I got up and tried to use my right hand which informed me in no uncertain terms I am still a cretin that tried to remove his fingers with a fan blade. It's right I am a complete tool! Thank god I still have a full set of fingers!
On that note have you ever tried to wipe your arse with your left hand? No? me neither until this morning and what an experience it is! It wasn't until I had lets say finished manoeuvres that as I sat there the dawning realisation of the task before me hit home. Its not really something you think about is it wiping your arse? I mean you just do it like so many other things it just has to be done... I ended up laughing at myself when I realised I was sort of hovering and balancing on my right leg whilst trying to aim my left hand with a safety "just in case this goes wrong" huge amount of loo roll thinking to myself "well which way do I normally wipe? Back to front, front to back?" It really isnt that complicated is it! Needless to say mission accomplished but my word it took some thinking about!

There was me thinking that brushing your teeth left handed was weird with the toothbrush facing the wrong way!

SO what could I do to the Landy today then? Obviously not a lot... I mean we know I am not allowed to do anything and after yesterdays near miss I wasnt up for pushing my luck too far, well that and my eldest daughter was kicking around the house in that semi awake state teenagers seem to live in and I am sure she was supposed to be at college so there may be a plot at keeping an eye on me going on here.

All I could come up with to do was to take the battery box cover out of the painting room (greenhouse) and fit it.

Looks good enough and has just shown me that I need to paint the inside of the Landy as well as the outside!

I then mooched around outside for a bit seeing a few things that "I could be getting on with" so quickly retreated indoors. Here I found in one of those cheesy gift magazines that kick around at Christmas time possibly THE most inappropriate gift I have ever seen...

FART PANTS. Pants that absorb the smell of your arse when you drop a doozy. Who thinks of these things? Who set up the photo of the bloke with his nose up the girls backside!??? If these places pay for stupid ideas I am going to be a very rich man!

min200

Re: The project has landed!

Seats!

Main
Posted by min200 Wed, November 19, 2014 15:50:27

Well my new seats have arrived! I say new but they are a set of "County" seats I bought off of a chap on Facewipe.
They are in great condition and will look the business when fitted.
They will be the last thing to go in as they are made of cloth and the front door windows are not completely water tight yet.
They are a bit flat from packing & postage but I shall leave them out in the dining room over night to puff back up a bit well until Wifey gets home and gives me some grief about that!
Being home this week does have some advantages!

easye1   19th-November-2014 18:51

Re: The project has landed!

very nice matey..
fingers in fans....may have told you already but..
my first born daughter followed me everywhere, including my garage/workshop of the time.
being a very hot summer i had a big fan going to move the air in/out but never had a cover on it.
i said to my 3 year daughter - DONT put your fingers near the fan....
turned round to hear screaming....
kids being kids done as they did and ended up with cut fingers....
shes 36`ish now and still has a go at me for having a fan without a guard..... lol..

min200   20th-November-2014 16:56

Re: The project has landed!

Well it WAS your fault chap LOL
A fan with no cover is about as daft as slipping your fingers into
metal blades spinning at 2000rpm.....I'll get me coat.

min200

Re: The project has landed!

Spare bolts.

Main
Posted by min200 Thu, November 20, 2014 16:52:04

I met up with the folk from the Nottingham Land Rover Club last
night at the pub and as always it was a pleasant evening with lots of
tall tales and laughter. My engine does run but is desperate for a
service and a bit of a tune up. Now give me a mini and I will do it
blind folded and I am sure tuning the engine and Carb is about the
same on the Landy but for the first go I really wanted someone
looking over my shoulder telling me I am doing it right or wrong
whatever the case may be. I found/bullied a volunteer to come along
with the bribe of cakes and chocolate so as soon as I am paid next
week I shall get the bits in and then we will be very nearly ready for
the MOT. Now I find myself wondering if I have done everything
right! I know there will be a few tweaks and the place I am taking ot
too will help me with those final tweaks before we put it in so that's
good. Dont want to fail on the brakes needing adjusting up a bit
more or the headlights pointing the wrong way!
The problem with the Landy sitting on the drive is the temptation.
Whatever window I pass it seems to sit there beckoning at me and
now the finish line is in sight I really do want to cross it as quickly as
possible! Obviously I am putting the brakes because a) Clumsy fat

sore fingers. b) I don't want to rush the last bit and spoil it by missing something simple or breaking something big.
Little bits then. I am running out of those this week those little things you can do with one hand. But I did remember that one of my wheels was leaking air so I rolled it out of the greenhouse and down to Wifeys car. Here I had to be careful because even though the inside of her car resembles a skip in the footwells most of the time (Im pretty sure most women are like this with cars...dirty buggers) she would be most unimpressed if she knew I was throwing a big land rover wheel in the back of it!

Cant see what the problem is myself...

The tyre was leaking air from the rim so the nice chap at the local garage unburdened me of the contents of my wallet to take the tyre off and give it a good clean up reseal and balance. That sorted and back I wondered what to do now and came up with the idea of loosening up the nuts on the drivers side window top ready for replacing with the better one in storage. I didnt know the strength of my left hand as I snapped the first one off but managed to a bit more gently persuade the second loose in one piece.

There are two things that for me are must haves in a rebuild. The first is a box of nuts and bolts that you have collected over time and thrown bits in "just in case"and a mixed box of washers as well...
Amongst these I found the two washers and bolts I will need to fit the new door top on saving myself a few pennies and a trip to the local ironmongers.
I then really wanted to change the tops over but my hand is healing nicely I have to go back to work next week if I want to eat and my fingers were warning me I had pushed far enough so I put the kettle on instead.
I did try to start my bike but it seems the battery has lost the will to live so that's a job for tomorrow. Autumn mornings are one of my favourites and with scenes like the last picture I took whilst walking the dog you must be able to see why!

Brown

Re: The project has landed!

Well, in some of the world's major civilisations and spiritual traditions you're supposed to wipe with your left hand anyway. Seems very awkward to me. Can't see how it caught on.

Good to hear the Land Rover is getting so close to completion.

min200

Re: The project has landed!

Would that the lost tribe of left handers??? Its just waiting to get messy lol

min200

Re: The project has landed!

New Shoes!

Main
Posted by min200 Fri, November 21, 2014 13:23:09

Had to go and collect a new battery for my bike first thing this morning as the old one has declared itself dead. So at the counter in the shop I tell the sales chap what battery I need and off he toddles and comes back with it asking "You do have a battery charger don't you?" Well why would I? so my answer is no. He then informs me it needs to be charged as they store them dry until they are sold when the acid is added. Is it just me or is this a bit odd? When you buy a car battery its charged and ready to roll so why wouldn't a bike one be the same?
I then asked him "Do you have a battery charger?" to which he replies with a grin "Yes yes we do" "good" I reply "Stick that battery on it and I will be back to collect it in the morning" The sales girl next to him burst into laughter and he toddled of back out to the

rear of the store muttering "ok then see you in the morning"
Back on the driveway in no time as the shop is just around the
corner I know I am going to potter a bit. I have cleaned out and
dressed my gammy finger this morning so I know I cant do too much
but I figure I can manage to fit the new front wheels. I set up with
the jack and wheel brace and my mobile rings with my middle
daughter calling me from her trip into London this morning to a
University interview. No let me point that out again...she is in
London. We go through the normal "Hellos" along with me saying
"Everything ok down there are you all right?" to which she replies
"Yea all good here....you are working on the Land Rover aren't you!
You are not supposed to be doing that!" How the hell do they know?
I hadn't even started just set up?? I have to admit I looked around
to see if they have set up a couple of cameras but cannot see any if
they have.

I told her I was "just looking at it" and promptly got to "looking" at
the old wheels being changed for the new again. There's nothing
really wrong with the old Series wheel rims that were on it but I
fancied a set of the early Discovery steel wheels with chunkier tyres
on.
With the front end still on axle stands the series wheels just fell off
so no hassle there but I had donned my babygrow so I could use my
legs to help manhandle the new wheels on.

Doesn't it look smart with its new shoes on!! I love it nice and chunky tyres and the matching Nato green looks a lot better on them than I thought it would. You could be forgiven if you are thinking I had forgotten to take out the axle stands from under the front but no they are gone!! It really sits that high up! I am loving the look of it even if I do say so myself!

I am happy to say the hand/axle/transmission brake works just fine the bricks are under the rear wheels as a "just in case" measure on my downhill driveway that leads directly onto the main city ring road. The last job of the day was to change over the rear number plate light. Yes I have done this once but since then I have managed to pick up a Land Rover one which looks a lot better than the truck one

I had stuck on before...I had a word with myself about being too much of a tight arse at times.
I need to update the project costings again but that can be done over the weekend.

min200

Re: The project has landed!

Spending

Main
Posted by min200 Sun, November 23, 2014 08:45:57
Talk about feeling sick. I had the shakes cold sweats and was distinctly light headed...I had to spend quite a large chunk of cash again.
You know the Landy is crawling closer to its first MOT and I am feeling a bit nervous about it if I am honest. The initial build is nearly done and it seems it will only be a few weeks before I get the insurance MOT and then send off for the age related number plates providing I have done my job right. Does anyone else worry that they have missed something? I am glad another landy nut is coming over to give it the once over before I book it in and he will definitely call me a tool and point out any shortcomings if I have made them. But this is not what has me feeling as bad as I do.
I have ordered all of the service bits which on a standard Land Rover is not too bad but for a 24v FFR the parts are a bit pricey to say the least. But it had to be done so the money is spent and all is ordered but the oil which I will go and collect myself from a little place down the road which is the rare oasis that is a reasonably priced car parts shop.
My other large outlay was a brand new fuel tank. As I have written

before the second hand unit I fitted is leaking and in all fairness the chap I bought it off of has dropped around another second hand one but I feel that seeing as I have spent this much so far on the project I may as well put my hand in my pocket one more time for the new fuel tank. Seems a bit excessive? With this large buy it now means I have replaced the fuel system up to the Carb completely so it shouldn't give me any more problems for some time to come.

Time for a bit of an add up on costs and they are crawling up considering I originally wanted to do this rebuild on a tight budget but as it was pointed out to me the other day how many other Land Rovers could you buy for that price with the new parts fitted and a rebuild being done to that extent? I also have the knowledge that it's all been done right (I hope!). When you look at it that way they are good points.

So with sweaty hands and a sick feeling in my stomach I have updated the costings...

Landy Project Costs

Land Rover £375

Sanding Discs £11.70

Ignition Barrel £20

Heritage letter £21.75

2x Batteries and rear 1/4 light £35

Pair Battery Terminal Clamps £3.99

Floor pan nuts & bolts £6.50

Grinding disc £2.25

Under Seal £8.99

Complete set of lights £85

5 Litres Primer £24.99

4 Discovery Wheels £10.20

Rear Door £21.00

Front Door £20.00

Handbrake spring £1.50

2 Discovery wheels

Two seatbelts

Wing Mirror

2 Headlight surrounds

2 headlight frames £60

2 Front Doors £60

Nato Green Paint £36

Rear Window Seal and insert £9.99

Wiring connectors £3.00

2 tins of silver metal paint £7.00

Fuses & Sandpaper £4.50

5x tins black spray £5.00

5x more tins black spray £5.00

Clutch fluid

Exhaust putty

WD40 £8.49

Car Boot Bits £13

Front & rear shocks £59.45

Front & rear brake rebuild kits £81.62

Fuel tank & filler £40

Wheels complete with tyres £250

Fuel pump

Fuel hose

Indicator stalk

Bonnet strap

Brake switch

Fuel pump gasket

Fuel line clips £67.74

24v Wiper motor

24v flasher relay

24v heater

24v front loom

oil cooler

Door tops x2

Rear bench seat £67.50

Roof rack £100

Wheel nuts £8

Brake pipe kit £39

Wheels & Tyres £250

Exhaust System & Flexi hose pipes £66

Number plate light £5

Seat set £90

Fuel tank and service parts £136

CREDIT FOR BITS SOLD OFF OF PROJECT £446

TOTAL £1616.16

That's a bit freaky..... £1616.16. Once the oil has been costed in and the price of an MOT we should be in the ball park of £1700 out of my own pocket and around £2200 all in with the bits taken off of the Landy and sold chipping in a good chunk of change.

For that sort of money and to me this is a lot of money I will have a cracking Land Rover that should last me a good few years before it wants a full rebuild again and that is not too shabby at all.

Discokids

Re: The project has landed!

Well I would be very happy with that. Excellent value for money!

aaronmorris

Re: The project has landed!

Quote:

> Originally Posted by Discokids (Post 3291477)
> *Well I would be very happy with that. Excellent value for money!*

Most definitely +1, I'm at about 5 times that!!
Own fault though :o

min200

Re: The project has landed!

5 times that!!!!!!!!!!!!!!!!!!!!!!!!!!! I would want a new one for that sort of money lol

I cant moan really :)

min200

Re: The project has landed!

Midweek Blues

Main
Posted by min200 Wed, November 26, 2014 07:44:14

Work really gets in the way of the fun things in life doesn't it. I came home last night to find a nice bog brown box waiting for me...
It contained the majority of my service bits for the landy as well as the nice shiny new fuel tank.
Its now Wednesday morning and as I sit here I realise that I have forgotten to order the oils...bugger. Well I guess I wont be doing that online now so I will have to run down to the cheap car parts store down the road as I first planned but I would have saved a few quid online...hey ho nothing I can do about that now apart from push back the service and set up but that is definitely happening on Saturday!
So I shall have to hide away my frustration at the lack of progress this week and make sure I get as much done as I can on Saturday.

Leebastard

Re: The project has landed!

i have just read your thread in its entirety. Superb sir, i applaud your work. id do however wish i hadn't read it in one go. and when did it become 2:30am? bugger.

min200

Re: The project has landed!

Quote:

> Originally Posted by Leebastard (Post 3293860)
> *i have just read your thread in its entirety. Superb sir, i applaud your work. id do however wish i hadn't read it in one go. and wher did it become 2:30am? bugger.*

LOL thanks for the compliment! This is the first time that someone has stayed up late for me in years LMAO

min200

Re: The project has landed!

Something just collapsed!!!

Main
Posted by min200 Fri, November 28, 2014 21:27:24

So I was eagerly heading home around the Nottingham ring road
banking left around a bend through some traffic lights and over some
cross roads when the front end of the bike just kinda gives
out...thankfully I was not travelling very fast but I took up both lanes
to recover it from going shiny side down and my first thought was
"front tyre blew out"
Nope the tyre is fine. I limped the poor old bugger home and the
bike too! The front end wobbling all over the shop but I was only a
mile away so a slow crawl at about 5mph saw me back soon enough
and safely to boot.
I grabbed a torch had a quick look and it would appear the frame at
the front is giving up the will to live. This is all in the dark so a closer
inspection in the morning will show to what extent it has gone BUT I
am sitting here at home with the Mrs having a beer and listening to
some tunes so life is still good. Wifey doesn't know why I am smiling
and being happy to still be in one piece she thinks the bike issue
wasn't such a big deal! Hey I don't care because I kept the bike
rubber side down...somehow.

Iann

29th-November-2014 14:40

Re: The project has landed!

glad your ok bud

You being a man of maturity and obvious good sense, would have
had full leathers boot gloves etc on to soften the blow i presume :)

min200

Re: The project has landed!

Yep always ride kitted up because I learnt that lesson the hard way about ten years ago and skinned arms from wrist to elbow that resemble red coloured cornflakes is not an experience I am in a rush to repeat!

Bike shopping now as its my transport to work....bloody hate shopping I am a man of simple needs and once I have something that works for me I keep it until it dies!

min200

Re: The project has landed!

Smug bugger.

Main
Posted by min200 Sat, November 29, 2014 17:43:24

Oh I am feeling like a proper smug bugger today. I had a friend call around who is a Land Rover nut and a good mechanic to boot. It was his first meeting with the old project and he was a mine of information. It turns out the Landy has had a recon engine installed because its a nice green colour and considering its only showing 24,000 on the clock anyway I wonder if they were changed at the same time or not? The timing and ignition are spot on so no worries there which has saved some buggering about. The words he seemed to use a lot this morning relating to me and the Landy were "bugger" as well as "Jammy". You see he really was impressed with the overall condition of just about everything so fingers crossed for the dreaded MOT.

After he left I still had an hour to kill before Wifey came home so we could go motorbike shopping and with the last electrical jobs niggling me I decided to have a stab at them again.

Now I am clueless when it comes to electrics but with this diagram of a 24v FFR wiring system in colour along with a multimeter set to the correct voltage even I was able to track back the wiring issues.

It is daunting though when you open up the centre consul and find a full on wiring mess lot looking at you.

I started to panic when I was finding wires like this lot!!!

But I took faith in the diagram and started to follow it back to get the horn working. I traced back from the relay to the change in wire colour testing for power at connections until I found out where the horn actually lived which is behind the grill on the nearside.

There was no power at the horn itself but there was at the connector on the offside by the headlight so through my cunning powers of deduction I realised the problem was between the two and quite obvious once I saw it...

"No way" I thought to myself "It cannot be that easy" after all we are talking Land Rover electrics here and they are a bain of every owners lives. I cleaned and connected the wires back up then turned on the ignition and pressed the horn....a dolcit grumpy sounding tone emitted loudly from the front end of the motor and the grin that spread across my face made my cheeks ache. Another electrical job down.

Could I beat that today? Could I get the rear fog lights to work or would I be removing them as they were not a legal requirement in 1983?

I grabbed my multimeter and diagram then attacked the wiring with gusto tracking the right colour through relays getting power all the way to the switch. Im getting into this electrical lark now you know.

The power died there so having seen the prices of a replacement 24v fog light switch I took to cleaning and WD40'ing (new word you know) it up then the moment had arrived to see if it had made any difference and whether I could crown myself the king of Land Rover electrics!!!!!!!!

Nothing.

I rechecked my work and pushed the spade connector into place properly and with the sounds of heavenly angels playing me soft music the most wonderful light came to life on the dashboard! That little yellow light on the top right held promise that the rear fog lights should be working and low and behold there was light!! I felt epic! The lighting system now works across the board on the old girl and the only electrical component to refit now will be the washer pump when I get a chance. Isn't it amazing how good you can feel when something new that you have learnt actually works out as it should. The way this is going I really may have this old mouldy Land Rover back on the road by the new year.

aaronmorris

29th-November-2014 22:11

Re: The project has landed!

Quote:

Originally Posted by min200 (Post 3292635)
5 times that!!!!!!!!!!!!!!!!!!!!!!!!!!! I would want a new one for that sort of money lol

I cant moan really :)

Exactly :eek: That's what I thought when I added it all up :o
Kind of scary really.
Me and my silly idea's!
Hopefully be worth it in the end!

min200

Re: The project has landed!

How much can you cram into a day?

Main
Posted by min200 Sun, November 30, 2014 19:58:53

I was up early. I just cant seem to have a lie in like other folk after 6
hours of snoring I wake up wide eyed and ready to start the day
whether I want to or not. After staring at the ceiling in the dark I lay
there determined not to get out of my pit until 7am. At 7am I was
just finishing my first cup of tea waiting for the light to come in
enough so I could potter outside on the Landy.
A bowl of cornflakes later and a play online the light was good
enough for the chickens to want to come out so it was good enough
for me to get myself into my baby grow and get stuck back into the
electrics. The washer bottle and pump were the last of my wiring
issues so I bolted them back into place, wired the washer pump up
filled the bottle full of washer fluid and wondered if my luck could
hold out for it to work.
It bloody worked!! I pushed the button the pump whirred into life
and the fluid worked its way through the pipework and squirted onto

the screen! Um that's all the electrics working then...I mean all of them the lot everything electrical on a Land Rover is operational. This must be a first on the planet and must be worthy of a prize of some sort!

That done its about 8am and the family are enjoying a lazy lie in and snoring away so I decided I would get the old leaky tank out and the new shiny one in place.
First I had to start taking the bits out of the tank.
The feeder pipe had to be swapped over as well as the fuel sender.
I then undid the four bolts that hold the tank in and that dropped out soon enough.
The new tank went in easy enough with the use of my jack to help balance it in place whilst I added the bolts to hold it in place. Soon enough it was done plumbed in and wired up. Being a tight git I drained the fuel out of the old tank checking it was clean and added back into the new tank. I should say here when I removed the fuel line from the old tank I folded it over itself and used a cable tie to stop any fuel leaking out.
Im glad I splashed out for a new tank because it should give me many years of service and that is the whole of the fuel system now replaced.

I fired it up and all is well in fact I love being able to turn the key when ever I want to and hear it running it never fails to bring a smile to my face!

By now the tribe were up and around and we had to head down south to look at a replacement bike. Don't you hate it when folk lie to you about the condition of a motor. This was supposedly on mint condition but after arriving it was scraped and scratched and dont get me started on the state of the nearly rusted through exhaust!
So a wasted trip of a 130 miles but we did call in on family and it was very good to see my baby sister and her fiancée back from Australia then we got fed a big fat roast to boot!
Now home and relaxing for a couple of hours wondering how the

weekend flew by so quickly and still looking for a bike.

www.justturned40.co.uk

lorri789

Re: The project has landed!

Excellent stuff. A Landy is a great way to spend spare time. Great blog too.

min200

Re: The project has landed!

Thanks glad you are enjoying the read :)

Loving the Landy myself and a excited the MOT is drawing nearer but kind of a bit disappointed the initial build is nearly done!

min200

Re: The project has landed!

Murky Mornings.

Main
Posted by min200 Wed, December 03, 2014 22:03:32

I am impatient to get this project done and I really don't want it to finish. You must have been there yourselves with something you have done at some point, you put in hours upon hours of effort relishing the challenge and hating the project at times. You sacrifice your pocket money the time you should have spent with the kids and offer up the odd limb or two in order to christen it with blood the Landy gods require if you want it to ever fire up into life again.

With December now upon us I have had a look at the calender for the month and to say the schedule is hectic would be a mild understatement. If I want to get any sort of time on the project it is in a small hour long window sometime from waking up to leaving for work. No really I am being serious! If I want any time to myself to do as I please I have that one option for most of the rest of the month....having a family seemed like such a good idea at the time!

Its amazing what you can do in a couple of hour long stints though. First I set to getting the old drivers side seat out. This is straight forward enough by simply lifting the base out and then folding the back of the seat forward. You will probably find that it doesn't want to go past the steering wheel of course but I found that just by moving the steering wheel from side to side a couple of times helped my "persuade" the seat back down. The single bolt removed from each side saw the back out pretty easily and quickly too.

That seat was pretty tatty and probably wont be any good for anyone but that wont stop me throwing it up onto fleabay on a free listing for 99p though! Hey any money back is a bonus and yes I am that much of a tight git...at times.

The seat frame was looking a bit rough...and I still had some green left so that got liberally splashed around the frame and rear bulkhead.

Onto the passenger side and that too was past its best so I got to splash it about a bit more.

It does make a hell of a difference a quick coat of paint even though I know these parts wont really been seen that often its nice to just "know" I have done it right.

I have bought off of the tinterweb a passenger side door top it as

brand new unused and seeing as I had to fit a new window kit to that side anyway I decided for the price of £15 I may as well "know" both of the door tops are new and that the glass wont be dropping out every tome I close the door like it does at the moment. The current passenger side door top is pretty rusty and will need a bit more exploration when its taken off to see if it would be worth keeping as a spare. The new one was the wrong colour so while I had the paint out...
Once the kit arrives I will get the glass in and tops changed over.

Next it was time to fit the windscreen wipers and I could not find them for love nor money. So after scratching my head and looking in many boxes along with all of my "safe" places I gave up and ordered a new pair convinced I had thrown them away by accident along with a load of rubbish out of the back of the Landy. The next morning I found them of course in plain sight on top of a toolbox. In my defence it wasn't a safe place toolbox and the mornings are very dull along with the wipers being very small and black.
Anyway it turns out I have two different types of wiper arms fitted to the Land Rover one being a series one and one slightly thicker one. A drill bit and some persuasion soon had both of the wipers fitted.

I think I will replace the arms at some point but I will get the MOT done first.

www.justturned40.co.uk

aaronmorris

Re: The project has landed!

Yes I agree, I think the project part of it is the fun part.
Probably why my neighbours hate me as I'll do as you've done, drive

it for 6 months, sell it and start again :o

min200

Re: The project has landed!

Normal Service Has Been Resumed

Main
Posted by min200 Sun, December 07, 2014 19:34:02

The bike crisis is over. I have picked up exactly the same bike as I own today so I can now get back to commuting as it should be done in a city. When I say exactly the same bike I do mean exactly the same bike! Its the same model year engine size and colour! What are the odds?
I was going to borrow some cash and spend a lot more and get something newer but when the same bike came up for £750 fully serviced with new boots battery exhaust system and my old bike sat there basically with every spare that I could need it was a win win situation.
The old bike will be stripped down and boxed up for the time being so I will have no worries of expensive repairs for some time to come!

My plan was to MOT the Landy by Christmas but the bike issue has out me back a couple of weeks on that plan. A turn up for the books is that Wifey has informed me that even though it looks like next Saturday was full of things to be done and visits to be made it is just for her and work friends so that leaves me with a full day to play with the project so maybe just maybe it could get an MOT before the new year.
I am not going to rush it though I want it done right but tis the time of year for miracles...

Discokids

7th-December-2014 20:51

Re: The project has landed!

Love the teapot, sounds well for the price. And having a complete bike worth of spares makes it great value. They're a better bike than people think.

min200

7th-December-2014 22:17

Re: The project has landed!

They are overlooked which suits me fine it keeps the price down. Same frame engine and wheels as a Bandit of the same age too which makes me laugh but hey why pay the extra??

Excellent cheap commuter bike ideal for the city!

davcud

7th-December-2014 23:02

Re: The project has landed!

Nice bike i had one a while ago

aaronmorris

8th-December-2014 09:38

Re: The project has landed!

I guess the bike is pretty good in the city centre.
We was working on the Victoria shopping centre their a few weeks
back and that was crap to get out of on a night.

min200   8th-December-2014 21:06

Re: The project has landed!

Quote:

> Originally Posted by aaronmorris (Post 3306286)
> *I guess the bike is pretty good in the city centre.*
> *We was working on the Victoria shopping centre their a few weeks*
> *back and that was crap to get out of on a night.*

Yep the city gets pretty much gridlocked daily so a bike is a
must here for me!

More Landy updates to come soon folks!

min200   9th-December-2014 21:26

Re: The project has landed!

Seat Back Bolts

Main

Posted by min200 Tue, December 09, 2014 21:25:32

It was bloody cold this morning in fact the Landy looked white and I was going to take some lovely Winter shots of it while I was out there but quite frankly I got sidetracked as usual and only remembered when I was on my way to work...typical.
This mornings reason for poking around the project was to see if I could find a couple of bolts that would fit into the passenger seat back so into the box of nuts and bolts I dived. When this search proved fruitless I remembered I threw loads of nuts and bolts into the spares big blue tub that was in the rear so I jumped in there and had a good sort out putting even more bolts into the right box of spares...success!
I found four bolts with the same thread pattern that along with a washer or two will fit so the seats should be in on Saturday :)
So I have a busy day planned while Wifey is off out with friends on the project including fitting seats, belts, changing oil and filters along with the spark plugs then last but not least fitting the new bonnet strap for the spare wheel on the bonnet.

Of course it will rain and spoil all of my fun...

www.justturned40.co.uk

easye1

10th-December-2014 08:49

Re: The project has landed!

nuts and bolts...
if you have a wilkinsons store near, have a peak to see if they do a plastic big you fill yourself of various nuts/bolts/washers all for about £3
I quite often pop into our store and think - what will I need

today.....lol

cant praise you enough of your everlasting log of enjoyable reading - "min"....

min200

Re: The project has landed!

Quote:

> Originally Posted by easye1 (Post 3308876)
> nuts and bolts...
> if you have a wilkinsons store near, have a peak to see if they do a plastic big you fill yourself of various nuts/bolts/washers all for about £3
> I quite often pop into our store and think - what will I need today.....lol
>
> cant praise you enough of your everlasting log of enjoyable reading - "min"....

Thanks fella! My Wilko's only does nuts and bolts in set bags :(

min200

Re: The project has landed!

Red Tape.

Main
Posted by min200 Wed, December 10, 2014 22:39:36

Well there I was getting all excited about being nearly at the MOT stage wasn't I but I thought I best give DVLA a quick call this morning just to confirm what they needed from me to register the Landy. I thought I had researched this part enough in the past but I am so glad I called because they came up with an extra chore I knew nothing about!

Firstly I shall start with what you will need to register any ex mod Land Rover and this is direct from the DVLA and correct on 10/12/2014.

V55-5 form. Fill this out ready for return.

Proof of age. This can be via the heritage museum or sometimes is supplied by Land Rover if you can convince them and will get you an age related plate.

A Photocopy of your Driving Licence and Passport.

Current MOT.

So you MUST have the above all ready to send off with a cheques for the £55 registration fee plus at least six months tax which in my case for a 2.25 petrol is £126.50.

Your vehicle must be insured on the VIN or DVLA will not process your application.

Don't get too comfy as we have not finished yet.

You will also need to contact HMRC to get confirmation that no import duties are owing on the vehicle.

They will send you some forms to fill out (sorry do not have the number for that one yet)

which you send back and four weeks later they tell you you owe nothing as it was built for the MOD and never officially exported BUT this does create a "NOVA" number that DVLA "Might" check upon your registration application.

Keeping up ok?

The exact words form the chap at HMRC were "Well this is a waste of time call DVLA back to make sure they want to do this as you have used the freedom of information act already and can prove what regiments this Land Rover was with so its never been exported"
I called DVLA back to be told "Well we might check with HMRC but we might not but we do most of the time unless you can send us documentation from the manufacturer to say it wasnt built for export"
"Err I have proof it was built for the MOD" I said
"But thats not the manufacturers" DVLA said.
"But its proof it wasn't built for export it was built for the BRITISH Army" I say.
"That's not on my list" says the DVLA chap "But it might be ok"
"Do DVLA work in "might be's"" I ask
"Sometimes but if it is not accepted by who looks at it your application will be denied within two weeks" DVLA said.

"So" I point out "Would it not just be easier for me to do the HMRC thing then as that only takes four weeks and if I try on a whim just sending you what I have now hoping its enough and its not that will put me back a fortnight"
"Yea probably" I get from DVLA now bored man.
The paperwork has been applied for and seeing as it will probably take at least two months not the one they say as its Christmas time there's no longer any great rush to get the Landy Mot'd and insured because most insurance companies will only insure the motor on a VIN number for 30 days!

I don't like wasting money so patience is a virtue here and seeing as its been this long in the making a bit more time wont hurt now. If you are doing your own ex MOD rebuild start the ball rolling on the paperwork quicker than I have!

Re: The project has landed!

Pillock.

Main
Posted by min200 Sat, December 13, 2014 17:54:48

I am starting today with the fact that I am stupid. I'm a pratt plonker tool dumb ass knobhead thick as two short planks not the sharpest tool in the box and of course a right pillock.
In fact calling myself those things is an insult to the people out there that are actually those things because my own stupidity has surprised even me. I had a realisation today whilst pottering around you know what its like you feel a bit smug and happy with progress and I was thinking how great it is that the Landy runs so well then the fact I didn't have to strip out seized clutch plates to make it move when I realised that this work of art I have been creating for myself just sits on my driveway.
When I say sits there I mean it sits on my driveway on the main ring road where everyone can see it day in day out, the Landy that now starts and drives. The Landy that I write an online blog about and any bad folk wouldn't hesitate to steal if they wanted the bits. The Landy that I have not been locking up or securing in any way...at all...even though its been running and has been drivable for a few weeks now.

That realisation woke me up I can tell you. You are always hearing of some scumbag stealing another Land Rover so I have made sure that my little project wont start run or be able to be driven away in any manner at all. Don't get me wrong if someone wants to steal something badly enough they will but hey why make it easy for the gits eh!

Anyway I had to start the day swapping a few bits over on the motorbikes mainly the exhaust system seeing as the new bike had a brand new Motad spanking exhaust on it that made it really loud reduced performance and was quickly getting on my nerves. On the standard system went and performance improved no end so I have a nice shiny exhaust gets to go on Ebay.

My attention then turned to the Landy. It was a tad on the cold side this morning.
I figured the best way defrost it was to see if it would start after a couple of weeks of standing which it did on the first couple of turns of the key! I love that arctic heater talk about toasty! First things first I wanted to get the drivers side door top swapped and the first nut came off no other but the second one had rusted through on the old top...
Out came the grinder to sort that little issue out and the new top soon dropped into place.
Then I wanted to get the seatbelts swapped over. I took out the drivers side one no problem just a couple of stiff bolts but a little WD40 and some brute force sorted them out. It was when I went to fit the nice Discovery ones I have had in my shed for months that the problem showed itself...
The original Series ones have a nice angle on the Latch arm but the Discovery ones are straight and bending wouldn't help because it twists at an angle as well. I'm a bit miffed as the fella who sold them to me sells lots of Land Rover bits and assured me they would fit straight in. Well they don't. Something else to add to the buy it list then.

Onto the seats then! I dug them out and fitted them drivers side first...
Then the passenger side...
So they are in. Nice to have seats again bit I am not sure if I like them! Still they will do for now funds are tight. On the subject of seats I need another back stop for the passenger side.
I am sure I had them all but I have either A) Sold them B) Thrown

them away C) Put them some where really really safe.

The HMRC NOVA form has arrived so I can have some fun filling that out later but it will get the ball rolling which is nice. I have revised my expectations for the MOT time and I don't think it will be until the end of January now weather pending of course.

Right gotta go as the kids are pestering me about putting up Christmas decorations now..no rest for the wicked eh!

www.justturned40.co.uk

min200

Re: The project has landed!

And that makes 100.

Main
Posted by min200 Sun, December 14, 2014 10:42:46

I'm sitting here just killing some time before we head off out for a family Christmas meal. You chaps know what its like it takes us 5 minutes to get ready including a shower and a shave then its an hour sitting about waiting for the woman or in my case women in your lives to finish preening pruning and hacking themselves about to look good while they are out to only then when they return wipe it all off and jump into slobby house clothes.
That has always seemed odd to me the whole "got to look my best" thing they do in case a complete stranger looks at them and judges them scruffy tramps but they are happy to turn into said scruffy tramps in front of us their life partners as soon as they are behind closed doors...go figure?

I suppose us chaps are just a different breed.

Well the great paper chase has begun with regards to getting the Landy registered with DVLA by filling out the Nova form for HMRC. Insomnia has struck me again and in all fairness it must be two or three years since it last came along to push my limits of normal functioning in next to no sleep for a week or so and what better way to utilise the time and try to make myself drop off than getting out of bed and filling out a form for the tax man!
As it turns out it is quite straight forward to do and I shall get it posted off to them today. The notes state that I will have an answer in within 14 days...it doesn't state what 14 days are they working days or the number of days from their receipt of them? Couple into that the fact it is Christmas time and I have never known any civil servant to work over the Crimbo New year period and the fact we are dealing with the tax man here and they really dance to the beat of their own drum so I should hopefully hear something back by mid January which will tie in nicely with getting the MOT sorted providing they have all the information they need in the first hit.

This is the 100th post I have done on the main blog forum Just turned 40. or www.justturned40.co.uk and I would like to say thanks to all of you who read it and thanks again for the comments you all send in and give to me both good bad and crazy! If anyone would like to get in touch directly you can email via Nick@nickysmith.me

Seems there are some stirrings from the top of the stairs so the tribe of women I live with must be nearly ready to leave and heaven help me if I am not ready to go once they have decided there is no turning back on the way they look because you never know what the next stranger might think of you....

min200   18th-December-2014 07:48

Re: The project has landed!

Slowing Down.

Main
Posted by min200 Thu, December 18, 2014 07:47:23

I am not as good as I once was of that there can be no doubt. I
know I am not old yet in fact I ma just starting out on middle age
and there are those that would argue that at 41 I have not even
started on that yet but I can confirm that I ache more easily these
days that I did before.
Progress has slowed on the Landy because, as I am sure I have said
before so forgive me for repeating myself, I have taken on the role at
work of "shunter" that gives me set day hours at work and which is
compiled of moving 60 trailers or so around the site at work which is
the size of a very large village and consists of getting in and out of
the "Tug" (like a truck cab) twice for each trailer and winding the legs
of the trailer up and down before and after its moved hopefully in the
right order so you don't drop the bloody thing on it's knees!
So for ten hours a day I get to do constant step aerobics along with
an upper body work out and this is as you can imagine not the most
mentally challenging role but it gives me set hours which as a HGV 1
driver is very rare and after three years of working into the early
hours of the morning and not seeing my family all week long is a
pleasant change! Oh and it keeps me fit whether I want it too or not.
Even a couple of years ago I would not have blinked at the physical
exercise of the role but even though I can keep the work up I now
ache like hell when I get in and it takes a good twenty minutes to
warm up my aching bones in the morning!
Another side effect is I only get the weekend to play on the project
and the next slot will be Saturday morning when I must get the
damned thing serviced properly before we have old friends arrive of
who my good friend the mechanic will be more than happy to escape

the woman chat that goes on endlessly for hours to play on the Landy with me so a polite cup of tea over twenty minutes should be enough before we excuse ourselves and leave the women to gossip and sort out lunch.

I have sent off the forms to the tax man for the NOVA number the DVLA want and have filled out the V55-5 form ready for despatch when the motor finally has its MOT. I hate paperwork so it's good to have it out of the way!

The project price list has not been updated for a while so here it is below adding bits bought and the taking away the last few bits sold off as well and I should have a bit more of an update on Saturday.

Landy Project Costs

Land Rover £375

Sanding Discs £11.70

Ignition Barrel £20

Heritage letter £21.75

2x Batteries and rear 1/4 light £35

Pair Battery Terminal Clamps £3.99

Floor pan nuts & bolts £6.50

Grinding disc £2.25

Under Seal £8.99

Complete set of lights £85

5 Litres Primer £24.99

4 Discovery Wheels £10.20

Rear Door £21.00

Front Door £20.00

Handbrake spring £1.50

2 Discovery wheels

Two seatbelts

Wing Mirror

2 Headlight surrounds

2 headlight frames £60

2 Front Doors £60

Nato Green Paint £36

Rear Window Seal and insert £9.99

Wiring connectors £3.00

2 tins of silver metal paint £7.00

Fuses & Sandpaper £4.50

5x tins black spray £5.00

5x more tins black spray £5.00

Clutch fluid

Exhaust putty

WD40 £8.49

Car Boot Bits £13

Front & rear shocks £59.45

Front & rear brake rebuild kits £81.62

Fuel tank & filler £40

Wheels complete with tyres £250

Fuel pump

Fuel hose

Indicator stalk

Bonnet strap

Brake switch

Fuel pump gasket

Fuel line clips £67.74

24v Wiper motor

24v flasher relay

24v heater

24v front loom

oil cooler

Door tops x2

Rear bench seat £67.50

Roof rack £100

Wheel nuts £8

Brake pipe kit £39

Wheels & Tyres £250

Exhaust System & Flexi hose pipes £66

Number plate light £5

Seat set £90

Fuel tank and service parts £136

Seat belts £61

Rear seat brackets £10

CREDIT FOR BITS SOLD OFF OF PROJECT £502

TOTAL £1631.16

www.justturned40.co.uk

easye1

Re: The project has landed!

good work min..
your mention of work equalls body wear is well know to myself.
last year while topped up daily with pain killers for my existing worn
hip & leg joint wear/pain all came to a crashing stop..to a point of
being unable to do much at all.
but then I was digging out tonns of essex clay in ground preporation
and concreting over a hand hammered hardcore base..
midway through the concreting the 50foot`ish driveway it all stopped
due to me being exhausted....
have always worked hard in work or play, but I was 65 last year.
took me best part of 10 months off to "get going again to finish all
the drive off to include the kids garden fence and increase the patio,
but, to be honest, my do or die attack on it all has left me more
disabled than before,
or is it because I am another year older. ??
being 40 is not a problem, being 45 or 55 or 65 is.....
your mind may think at being a 40 year old, but dam sure you body
cannot keep up at 66....lol

love to read your updates min....
but maybe think of a lump of chain wound round your brake and
clutch then passing through your steering wheel as a precaution
against theft eh.. plus maybe one of them round steeringwheel disc
locks too....
the landie is becoming a great thing to own, so make it harder for
someone else to own it eh..

min200

18th-December-2014 20:25

Re: The project has landed!

Feeling a bit worn on places now chap and it sounds as if we are cut from the same cloth! I just plod on with something until its done work wise and then my body just say..."Really?" then I pay for it lol.

The Landy is now well secured but I shall not post exactly how ;)

min200

Re: The project has landed!

Festive friends.

Main
Posted by min200 Sat, December 20, 2014 20:19:47

Crazy busy today on the Landy :) Wifey buggered off out first thing this morning to spend more money than I want to know about on Christmas treats before our friends were due to arrive at lunchtime so I managed to jump straight into my babygrow grab a wolly hat because it was bloody cold out there this morning and get stuck into the niggly jobs that had been grating at me for a few weeks.

First up was changing the spark plugs and being 24 volt the set up is a bit different so I loosened the leads on the end of the plugs using an adjustable spanner because for the first time in this rebuild I have not had the size needed in either of my toolboxes so that has been added to my "I want" list. That was the first problem and I soon arrived at the second one. After liberally dosing up the old spark plugs happily they came straight out but it was immediately apparent that I have bought he wrong plugs to fit...
See the difference was in the bottom of the plugs and to think the chap who sold me them at the Peterborough show was so adamant that they

were the correct ones! Oh well whats done is done so I will now have to find out the correct part number for them.

The old ones are rusty to say the least and left a pile of rusty gunk right at the top of the spark plug hole on the head.

Now that lot was just waiting to fall into the piston chamber and being in a really deep ingress I pulled out my trusty magnet on an ariel stick to help fish the crap out...

If you have not got one of these in your toolbox I suggest for a couple of quid you grab one because I have used this old thing so many times I have lost count!

I have popped the old plug back in and nipped everything back up again because even though they are rusty on the outside they work and will keep any moisture out of the piston chambers.

Then it was onto the oil and a quick drain down of the old mucky stuff by removing the sump plug first of course and it was then onto removing the oil filter from the housing which is ccunninglydesigned to be in such a place that it is really awkward to get off without getting oil all over the shop!

I undid it a few turns until the oil just started to dribble out into the tub and left it like that for a few minutes until the worst of it had gone into the bucket instead of all over me then took the housing off binned the old filter, fitted the new and refit again. In went 6 litres of oil and I then found my batteries were flat....so they have been put on charge until tomorrow.

Then in perfect timing my friends turned up (yes I do have real life ones you know...not many admittedly but I am rather picky about folks who do my nut in and chat shit) so it was time for tea and biscuits until Wifey returned home. She wasn't long so us men folk retired back out into the cold like the hunter gatherers we are and had another pop at the project.

I soon put the good fellow to work fitting the new spare wheel strap onto the bonnet.

The bonnet needed a new front rubber bung for the wheel to sit on.

Well don't go paying the stupid prices the spares folk want for a a new set just order yourselves a set of 40mm x 10mm rubber suitcase feet for the princely sum of £2.99 delivered! Keep an eye out because you will see where the rest were used shortly. Once the strap was fitted I grabbed the spare wheel and put it into place with a very sturdy padlock to stop the scumbags...

Now it's on I think I would like a plain black cover for it as well...added to the list as well now but is not needed for the MOT so will have to wait.

Lunch was at this point forced upon us so we came into the warmth for good food and better company, I love catching up with true friends you know the ones you may not have seen each other for months or years but when you meet up it was like you saw each other last weekend. So after a lot of laughter and with full bellies we ran away from the washing up declaring we were in the middle of something important that had to be done on the Landy (I WILL need another excuse once this is finished to keep running away from the washing up. Suggestions via email please) and decided that the seatbelts just had to be fitted.

I set my friend on with that while I fitted the replacement seat back supports on the drivers side and those suitcase feet are back again put onto the ends of the supports! Well I did have to buy a set of four so why waste more money buying the official land rover rubbers? These will work just fine!

I tidied up some loose ends in the back refitting the rear light panels that have sat in the tubs since I played with the wiring. How confident am I that the electrics are now sorted that I am putting covers back in place....give it a week and they will probably be off again! The very last bit of underseal went onto the chassis where the passenger side fuel tank was removed and this is a job I have been putting off for months...bloody black awful stuff that it is and how do I always without fail end up bathing in the stuff? There is not that much of it in the damned can!

The seatbelts were soon fitted (gotta love having a proper mechanic working with you) and they are looking good!

At this point the sun had gone down so I knew it was time to call it a day outside. So we forced ourselves to pack away and soon learnt that we had just missed watching the film Frozen....the Landy gods were being kind today.

More food and more laughter were the ingredients of the late afternoon which has set us into a very festive mood. More Yuletide food with the extended family tomorrow which will be nice as I am the eldest of six children and for the first time in many years we will all be in the same place at the same time for a seasonal meal.

So this I expect will be my last post before the Christmas holiday so I would like to take the opportunity to say to you all please have a great Christmas however you celebrate it whether that's at home staying out of the way of it all or travelling to see your families. Enjoy the laughter or the peace smile at a stranger and say hello to a friend.

Merry Christmas everyone and I will see you on the other side.

easye1   20th-December-2014 21:33

Re: The project has landed!

a happy restive period to you too min ;)

elan23   21st-December-2014 15:44

Re: The project has landed!

Plugs look the same as the new plugs I have bought for my 24v lightweight, they havea special tip or summat, can you post the plug number and I will check with mine tomorrow.
Regards, Peter.

min200

Re: The project has landed!

I will have to dig them out Peter but the ones I need are RSN12Y I am told and they look the same as mine!

Merry Christmas :)

elan23

Re: The project has landed!

Mine are RSN13P (I guess the P stands for platinum) and they look the same as your new plugs. If in doubt then try first and see how it runs, a plug chop would not come amiss.
Regards, Peter.

min200

Re: The project has landed!

Building and Bumps.

Main
Posted by min200 Sat, December 27, 2014 18:45:17

Well it was a nice Christmas day the kids were happy and so was Wifey then best of all the traditional visit to the mother in law was cut to a 30 minute stint...beat that! (I do her no justice here she has a heart of gold and yes I am being held at gunpoint here)

But the only day off I get is Christmas day because I work for a large multi national that worships the retail gods and you only get Christmas day off because they have to give it you. Remember when the shops were shut for a week at a time? I loved that as a kid and it is with a heavy heart I realise that my kids will never experience such things. Enough with the melancholy I am warm well fed (a bit too well !) and live in a place that offers a good life so I shall stop moaning for times gone by.

Boxing day started well with a good ride to work enjoying the seasonal lack of cars on Nottingham's ring road and the day was a steady plod on with even my work colleagues being somewhere near to normal breathing everyday folk instead of the usual bunch of "what the hell can we find to moan about today to anyone that will listen to my crap because being miserable and making others feeling the same is the only source of enjoyment I can find in life any more" chaps they usually are, Christmas was truly in the air! About 5pm it started to rain...heavily...nothing unusual about that I just donned my wet weather gear and carried on. I had not seen the weather forecast for the day. It started to snow. Nothing too bad just wet stuff that melted as soon as it landed so I carried on. Before I realised 20 minutes later I noticed the snow settling and settling well at that...I made a call into the office..."It's snowing like hell out here settling well and I am on a motorbike so I am off now!" Again it must have been the Christmas spirit about because no one complained about me leaving 30 minutes early...I wish I had left an hour before that.

I kid you not it took me ten minutes to get my gear on and clock out
by which time the snow had settled well and was coming down in
proper blizzard fashion. As I walked outside I had to wonder at my
sanity of getting onto the bike but I didn't want to get Wifey out in it
after spending the last 15 years experiencing her driving in ideal
conditions I convinced myself that the main roads would be ok. I
mean I live in a major city that is travelled well by lots of traffic and
has a mass of gritters on hand so the ring road I had to travel 8
miles on should be just fine. First I had to travel the mile to the ring
road though....I nearly made it...it was 3 inches deep in snow and I
could see the finish line of the ring road entry just 50 feet away
when my world started to look kind of strange. Seeing as I was only
doing 10 mph I did what can only be described as the best ever slow
motion fall off of a motorbike in the history of bike crashes. First I
realised of any sort of problem was when the horizon appeared to be
vertical then what can only be described as a falling into a mound of
feathers as I impacted onto the road. The bike went left up a kerb
and I slid in a nice comfy line creating the longest snow angel in
history. Feeling like a right pillock I got to my feet walked back the
15 feet to my bike and with the help of the kerb picked the bloody
thing up.

At this point you are thinking "why would you get back on it?" I know
you are because in hindsight I thought the same thing but I was
convinced the ring road would be alright and I put my faith in the
local councils ability to keep the roads passable. In my defence I had
just fallen off of a bike and banged my head was running on
adrenaline and was getting colder than I realised really quickly. The
old girl started again and I set off like a kid with both feet down
riding at 5mph.

I didn't get above 10mph for the next hour. The ring road was ok to
start and better than the side road had been but it was still bad. My
visor steamed up in 30 seconds flat. My glasses then froze in another

two minutes so I pulled over and took them off. Then I had to convince myself I was a brave man and carried on off into the storm. At this point the road was turning white and the blizzard was blowing directly into my face. God knows what I looked like squinting like I needed to have some glasses on (I did) with frozen eyebrows and frozen snot down my beard with my feet down either side because I didn't want to fall over again whilst riding next to the gutter on a major ring road at 10 mph but it couldn't have been half as bad as I felt.

This was the singular worst riding experience of my life and I have ridden for years all year round in just about all weathers but I will never ride in the snow again.

I nearly made it home.

I was less than a mile away, just, but there was a roundabout and the blizzard was in full flow.

I nearly made it around it.

The off was quick and I mean real quick maybe it was because I was near frozen at this point or the fact I could barely see right anymore because of the storm or the fact I was exhausted that I didn't realise I was off until I was sliding into the third exit. The motorbike had left at the second exit leaving me to carry on by myself I think it had had enough as well. I lay there thinking "ok then that was a good bump" knowing I hadn't broken anything but knowing I was going to hurt in the morning.

The first four cars just steered around me lying in the road and carried on their way....arseholes...but then my faith in humanity was restored as a nice couple pulled up behind me with their hazards on and helped me up. Then by a quirky coincidence an ambulance pulled alongside them with lights flashing and helped me pick up the bike whilst blocking the roundabout completely. Sorry if you were stuck behind me for a few minutes but that was far better than me getting run over...I am a selfish git like that.

We blokes don't know when to quit do we. We don't like going to the Dr's we push on when we shouldn't we don't like making two trips from the car with the shopping. We see it as a challenge and we accept that challenge because we are the hunters the gatherers and the protectors. We do not like to admit defeat.

I quit.

I had got to my breaking point with my nerve the cold and I periodically could not face falling off of the bike again. I had been lucky twice and any "off" of a bike you walk away from is a good one. I dumped the bike on the pathway and hiked the last of the journey home through the storm and quite frankly with all that moving it was the warmest I had been for what felt like hours.

When I hit my driveway I was greeted by this sight...

Looks good eh! Like it should be out and about in the snow...wish I had already finished the rebuild and registration!

I awoke with some really impressive bruising and collected the bike this morning but instead of snow it was ice to dance with fate seems to enjoy having a laugh at the moment at my expense.
I'm glad to say no real damage done to either the bike or me but once I got back in today I have spent the rest of it building a massive dolls house that my youngest daughter got for Christmas and if I am honest I think I may just stay in nursing my bruises all weekend and watching the weather forecasts.

v8geoff

27th-December-2014 19:30

Re: The project has landed!

Looking good matey

min200

27th-December-2014 19:48

Re: The project has landed!

Quote:

> Originally Posted by **v8geoff** (Post 3326998)
> *Looking good matey*

Thanks fella nearly there now :)

Discokids

27th-December-2014 20:44

Re: The project has landed!

Sorry to hear about your off Min, I once (about 10 years ago) rode my bandit 600 2 up home from Scarborough to ilkeston in the snow, 5 hours it took, was settling on the m1. Dropped at the bottom of my street even though we had FOUR feet on the ground! Said I'd never ride in the snow again.

Anyway, the landy looks mighty fine with that snow all over it.

Re: The project has landed!

I agree I will never ride with snow on the ground again either but unfortunately it's not my first off but I walked away so all good there.

Bloody sore all over now though lol

Re: The project has landed!

Bike tires + snow never works. I've done exactly the same but I've had that same 'get home' feeling. Landy looks great, just wait till you get that first drive.

Re: The project has landed!

I know cannot wait to get it on the road!

min200

Re: The project has landed!

Hard Frost & Heaters

Main
Posted by min200 Sun, December 28, 2014 15:07:42

I would love to be able to play in the snow with my old Landy and that time should come soon enough so today with aches and bruises from Friday nights adventures I thought I might mop a few of the little outstanding jobs on it.
An early Christmas present arrived on Christmas eve in the form of four replacement spark plugs of the correct spec for my old motor. I was amazed at this because I had only ordered them the day before so how on earth they made it to me so quickly during the Christmas rush I do not know but I was happy to see them.
It wasn't until today that I managed to get around to fitting them and I was pleasantly surprised that the old plugs and leads came out and off with no issues at all. These normally make all sorts of strange sounds when I am involved and I have even had the odd plug snap off in the head on me in the past but I was one step ahead on these ones as I had soaked the buggers in WD40 a week ago and left

puddles of the stuff in the spark plug recess to soak in...it worked a treat!
So it was out with the old and in with the new....

A turn of the key and the engine fired into to life and seems to have lost the worst of the odd misfire it had before which is nice so I left it ticking over and thought I would see how quick the Artic heater would warm the motor through which it did in a matter of minutes so hopefully I wont be victim to the normal frozen winter feeling that most Landy drivers suffer from...what a smug git I will be!

Seeing as this was going so well I decided I better get the passenger door top fitted that has been kicking around for a while. Better to play indoors with this though so I snuck the top window and the runners that needed to be fitted into the dining room like a ninja on a mission as Wifey was distracted by some girly film on the box. The first she realised what was happening was when I was drilling the pilot holes for screwing the runners in but by then I was in and refusing to go and play in the cold again until I had to!

With everything laid out I got stuck in and once it was built I headed out into the frost to fit it but of course the old bolts wouldn't let go so I then had to drag out the grinder along with 50 feet of extension cable to do two ten second cuts. There was a sizzle as the old bolts dropped into the snow and the new one dropped straight into place. The old wreck is now wind proof and water tightish which pleases me no end :)
Looking for something to do I then found a pair of old mesh light covers I bought months ago put at the back of the shed and promptly forgot about so this was a nice surprise or the early onset of dementia who knows. I remembered that I wanted to spray these black so I grabbed a can of poundland special and set to work.
They look good but I wont be fitting them until after the MOT as the headlights need adjusting so best keep that easy access just in case well that and I will probably forget about the light guards again and find them in a few months which will be a nice surprise for the future me.

All that is really left is to secure the batteries now so I best be getting the transport to the MOT centre sorted out.

justturned40.co.uk

Discokids

28th-December-2014 17:19

Re: The project has landed!

Transport????

min200

Re: The project has landed!

Quote:

> Originally Posted by Discokids (Post 3327901)
> *Transport????*

Yep I am still waiting for the tax man to tell me I owe nothing on import duties...crazy eh! So I don't want to insure it on the VIN plate yet as you only get 30 days to get the registration number from the DVLA which I cannot get until the tax man gives me the all clear and a NOVA number to say so to the DVLA who then in turn will want it insuring once that is done so they can register it but God only knows how long it will be before the Tax man says its ok because we have had Christmas and New Year and as we all know civil servants do like a very long winter holiday so I don't want to waste my money insuring the old motor more than once because it's taken longer than 30 days but would like to get the MOT done so it can be registered...

And breathe.

Discokids

Re: The project has landed!

Oh.

min200

Re: The project has landed!

Quote:

> Originally Posted by Discokids (Post 3327961)
> *Oh.*

That my friend is the best reply ever! LMAO Superb!

Pcwizme

Re: The project has landed!

So I have read the compleate story in one sitting and all I can say is fully respect to you, from what looked like a lost cause, to a beautiful machine... and how little money it cost is amazing! Well done sir!

min200   29th-December-2014 07:45

Re: The project has landed!

Well thank you! Being a tight arse helps to keep the cost's down on the project ;)

In all seriousness I have surprised myself across the board if I am honest!

min200   31st-December-2014 19:59

Re: The project has landed!

HAPPY NEW YEAR!

Main
Posted by min200 Wed, December 31, 2014 19:58:29

Happy New Year to everyone!

I hope that whatever you are doing tonight brings you a bit of joy and may 2015 give you what you deserve :)

Enjoy the night and may your hangover be short...I'm straight back to work in the morning so a dry night for me :(

Aveling11956

Re: The project has landed!

Just read this thread from the start and all I can say is well done you have done an amazing job!

min200

Re: The project has landed!

Quote:

> Originally Posted by Aveling11956 (Post 3332731)
> *Just read this thread from the start and all I can say is well done you have done an amazing job!*

Thanks for that I'm glad you are enjoying the read :)

I'm really chuffed with it and cannot wait to get it on the road now then more tales from it will be told I'm sure ;)

www.justturned40.co.uk

mick2a

Re: The project has landed!

This has made what was a dull day bright again. Thanks for a great read and well done. Hope you get it on the road soon.

Mick.

min200

Re: The project has landed!

Cheers Mick! Hopefully on the road again within a month or so so keep reading :)

min200

Re: The project has landed!

Frozen

Main
Posted by min200 Thu, January 01, 2015 18:55:40

No not the bloody film that even though my kids have now grown up they and Wifey love for some reason and seem to be happy to sing the same songs over and over and over again. No by the title

"Frozen" I refer to my poor bugger of a project that sat on the driveway not getting any sunshine doing it's best impersonation of an ice cube since Boxing Day.

Seeing as my work so generously let us leave work today once all of the little work we had to do was done on this the first day of 2015 I thought I best see if the old motor would start up or whether the batteries might need a charge.

I kid you not it started on the first turn of the key. I have had modern motors that never ever started on the first turn the whole time I owned them! This got me to thinking....this project of mine was "Demobbed" in 1998 and basically sat around from that point until I bought it early 2014...that for the rubbish at math to save you taking your socks off to count your toes is 16 years.

16 years of Spring Summer Autumn and most importantly Winters. I seem to recall a couple of years ago we had "The worst winter ever" where we were all snowed in and chilly for a couple of months and this old motor just sat through it with no one paying it any mind let alone attention or care. So it has frozen and thawed then been cooked and soaked without turning a wheel or a cog for year upon year then when I get it it gives a shrug and fires up like it was serviced regularly the whole time.

Don't suppose I should worry about a nippy week with it then seeing as it is a brilliant bit of engineering and by all accounts far tougher than I will ever be!

www.justturned40.co.uk

min200   3rd-January-2015 19:13

Re: The project has landed!

Taps & Tights

Main
Posted by min200 Sat, January 03, 2015 19:08:11

I got conned like a novice today. I mean I have been with Wifey for 15 years and around the block a fair few times before that so to fall for something as simple as "I just need to pop into here to buy a dress" I deserve everything I got.

See this picture here chaps.....

These are the gates to Hell itself. If you look closely there is a red sign in the middle of the windows proclaiming what torture you are in for if you dare to enter but did I notice this before losing my soul this morning? I am sorry to say chaps I did not I fell for it hook line and sinker. "A dress" I fear not my friends it was not just a dress...it was many dresses in fact it was more dresses than I have ever seen collected into one place just to increase the torture for the men who unsuspectingly walk in with their women. Oh I haven't finished on the torture front yet I was repeatedly asked by Wifey if I liked this dress or that dress and why was I looking so fed up didn't I like her in any of the dresses what was I trying to say what was the matter with me shouldn't she look nice for me?

Sweet Jesus there is no other no win situation like watching your woman drive herself into a frenzy over clothes like a demented nutjob then have all of that pent up what I think is excitement aimed at you! I dutifully sat outside the changing rooms making the right noises after having being paraded an unknown number of outfits when I figured a way out...

Say you have a "windy" stomach and need to go outside for "a walk" to let nature take it's smelly course. It worked! Then the cherry on the cake was the discovery of a huge motorbike shop around the corner!

I managed to kill an hour looking at gear I need to replace this year and sorting a few prices out on my head. When I headed back toward the gates of hall I decided a phone call would be better than actually walking through them voluntarily again then twenty minutes later I was happily driving away with Wifey stored on board along with several new frocks...I believe they were the first three she had looked at as soon as we arrived but hey what do I know?

My prize when I got home was on hours peace to play on the Landy while she tried all the clothes on again but hey I was happy to escape for a while. There was only really one big outstanding job left and that was to sort out the battery brackets.

I bought two pairs of universal battery arms and clamps a while back now but when they arrived I realised I had made a cock up size wise and these ere way too long with the thread finishing about 2 inches short of where they were needed to actually hold the batteries in place! A friend at work had a tap & die set I could borrow so I set to sorting these extra long bars out.

First I cut them to the right size and set to starting off the right thread size. I found it best to wind forward and back until the thread was about 10mm long then it was a straight cut down to where I needed the thread to end.
This was my first go at this and I was surprised how easy it went four times over beginners luck maybe? All the wing nuts fitted fine as well so I will be securing the batteries in the morning and with that chore done the old Landy will be ready to be sent off to for MOT at the end of the month by witch time the Tax Man should have told me all is ok import wise, as in it has never been exported or imported so I owe no money, and then the docs can go off to the DVLA which can be another kettle of fish!

Still first things first lets get the MOT sorted which I would love to do next Friday as I am off work but I dont want to insure it yet because you only get 30 days to then get it registered properly or it costs a fistful more cash. That is of course unless anyone is kicking about with trade plates or a big trailer and has nothing better to do then otherwise patience will have to prevail and the use of the very kind offer of transport I have at months end that will save me lots of money will do quite nicely :)

justturned40.co.uk

min200
4th-January-2015 16:58

Re: The project has landed!

It's Ready...

Main
Posted by min200 Sun, January 04, 2015 16:50:02

Um I can't quite believe I am about to say this after 8 months or so
of hard work but I think the Land Rover is ready for its MOT.

Remember when it looked like this...

Doesn't seem very long ago and in the grand scheme of things I
suppose it is not and I have thoroughly enjoyed myself on the
rebuild so much in fact I think another one will have to be done at
some point but I best not get ahead of myself just yet seeing as I
still need that all important MOT and registration plates. I have just
surprised myself that I managed to do it all without killing myself or
at the very least losing a limb or two. I suppose I have missed
something and they will point it out and laugh at me while printing
off the MOT failure sheet but I think I have covered all the bases.

The last few bits of pottering around on it today have been fun and had a kind of a feeling of finality about them as they were the odd's and sods I had either put off or forgot about repeatedly. I started by rebolting (is that a word?) the oil cooler exchange back onto the inner wing and then I bolted the Artic heater feeder pipe back into place below the oil cooler.

With those done I pumped up all of the tyres to the correct pressures and set to cleaning the dash and cab out it was nice to see the plastics all shiny and black again! I used good old WD40 to bring back the shine. Then it was the turn of all the junk out of the back along with a sweep and it came up quite nicely.

I bolted the batteries into place with the newly threaded bars I did yesterday and then wondered what else I had to do. I remembered a mechanic friend had told me I needed to move the ladder on the back to the offside so it didn't block the view of the numberplate when it is fitted but quite frankly after grinding off old bolts and fitting the ladder into place with new ones it seems to be more of a pain seeing the lights now on the offside but hell I will just let the MOT chap tell me when I am there and remove it if I need to.

By now I was really scratching about wondering if I had missed anything else and I decided to fit the new CB into place that I got for Christmas. The Ariel wiring has been run along the old radio wiring route using existing clamps to hold it into place which saved a lot of buggering about! Seeing as the mounting holes were on the wings for the old radio kit I decided to use one of those on the nearside wing to mount the new black ariel into place.

I think it looks quite good there just like it belongs. But where to mount the CB radio itself? I held it in place on the top of the dash but didn't like it there. Under teh dash then that would look ok wouldn't It? Nope didn't like it there either. Was I being too picky at this point? I don't know but every spot in the front of the cab just felt wrong. I turned around to look out of the back door when an idea I liked hit me.

It's my Landy right so I thought yea that could be just the spot lets go all Smoky and the Bandit with it. I mounted the radio between the seats. Then I mounted the mike above my head on the tubing that houses the heater pipes up high so I can just reach up and "Ten Four good buddy!"

I still need to fit a 24v-12v dropper before I wire it into the electrics but that can be done once the MOT is sorted best save all my pennies until then in case I have missed something.
So that's it until I get it in and that depends on what the tax an says but I will call a couple of insurance companies tomorrow to see what can be sorted if I exceed there 30 day limit on taking the policy out to getting the registration plates from the DVLA.

min200

Re: The project has landed!

Booked in...

Main
Posted by min200 Wed, January 07, 2015 22:25:18

There's no stopping me now I have realised that I think the Landy is ready for it's first bash at a ticket. The insurance has been bought with a 60 day leave of absence to get the registration sorted and the MOT is booked for this Friday at 10am.
I have to be honest I must have missed something here there WILL be something it fails on if not several some things so I am treating Friday as a "Oi knobhead don't you think you should fix this first before it goes on the road?" sort of appointment that will give me a list of niggly bits to sort out by next weekend when I will take it back for a retest should it fail.
So why do I feel a little bit nervous then? Why are there butterflies in my stomach when I think about driving it to the test centre and

waiting while some other bloke has a poke around with my project? Am I jealous that another man is going to get intimate with it and am I just excited to be driving it finally or terrified that it wont make the 2 mile drive each way? I have even sorted out a recovery plan in case it goes wrong in the form of a mate with another 4x4 and a rope to get me home so there every eventuality has been covered really so this should in theory make me more settled but it doesn't.

9 months hard work is in the firing line here and I think the biggest issue is I don't want someone else telling me it's crap even though I know it isnt! So time to suck it up take it in and see what happens the report will be online by Friday evening but it may be a little tear stained...

Here's secretly hoping!

Discokids   7th-January-2015 22:48

Re: The project has landed!

Good luck for the test, don't think you need it but hope it goes through.

txGeek   7th-January-2015 23:17

Re: The project has landed!

That is some outstanding work right there! From Beast to Beauty.

Would love to get as lucky on that find!
Bill

easye1

Re: The project has landed!

good luck min..
as you can see i is back here again...

very addictive reading your blog..

min200

Re: The project has landed!

Thanks everyone I suppose we shall see in the morning eh!

Huddy84

Re: The project has landed!

All the best! Have confidence. I was surprised when mine past, before I noticed it was with no advisories.

Discokids

Re: The project has landed!

Well????

min200   9th-January-2015 16:08

Re: The project has landed!

Well what?

min200   9th-January-2015 16:12

Re: The project has landed!

LOL ok then...

Well it went for MOT...

Main
Posted by min200 Fri, January 09, 2015 16:07:51

Why do I worry myself sick over things I cannot control with motors?
I don't do it with motorbikes if they break I fix them and go on again
then the ludicrous thing is if a car breaks I fix and drive away again
but for some strange reason cars worry me. They worry me in the
way that I think they are always "about to" break and after
thousands of faultless miles they eventually do and I think to myself
"see there it's broken it's let me down!" without thinking about all
the trouble free motoring it's done.
So with that in mind can you imagine what I was like this morning
before setting off in the Landy? I have NEVER driven it further than
six feet forwards or backwards in a straight line so I was worrying
about whether the steering would fall off when I went around a
corner? (I know stupid right) would the engine run ok under load?
(even though I have revved the nuts off of it on a regular basis on

the driveway) would the gearbox collapse? (why would it?) are the propshafts straight? Oh my God is the tracking ok enough or will it pull me up the neighbours driveway as soon as I leave? (I am working myself up into a frenzy now) it was at this point my body said to my head "time out now you are going to stop pacing and sit down for a bit".

I didn't faint or pass out but as I sat on the toilet in a smell that quite frankly made me feel sick even though it was my own I attempted to take some deep breathes quickly put that down to a bad idea due to the stench and got my mind back under control. Test time had arrived so with a new found stoicism I jumped into the drivers seat prayed it would start which of course it did and set to taking the project for it's first proper drive in 16 years. It drove as it should in a nice straight line with soup bowl gear changes rattling away nicely and being generally very very loud. After the first two corners and a roundabout I had forearms like Popeye (if you don't know who Popeye is Google it then be thankful you are still very young) the brakes needed a second pump to grip really well as they settled in and the temp gauge sat at normal. Two miles and a stomach churning 5 minute drive later we arrived at the test centre to the owners remark of "I thought you had rebuilt mate" Funny bugger.
I should point out at this point if you are registering a motor after it's MOT like me take all the paperwork you have to the testing station with you because it makes these guys a lot easier when entering the details. The most essential info was the proof of date of build letter I had that info was like gold when setting up the test itself.

Time to go into grown up bloke mode and not show the panic in my eyes as they took it inside the doors. I stood pacing up and down like an expectant Father in fact I don't recall being that worried when the kids were being born but I suppose I was really doing the work then eh I had already done my bit! It was now over a pit...

They left the engine running longer than it has ever run before and much to my surprise it didn't dump it's coolant everywhere at any point! They were extremely thorough though in fact I thought they were far more thorough than I had ever been on my driveway during the rebuild but that was just doubt talking.

These guys were knowledgeable as well they knew that it was not a "handbrake" but a transmission brake and to test them off they set with the tester thing (forgot to ask what it was called so forgive me but I was far too busy worrying to remember everything!) you put in the passenger floor well when driving to make sure the brakes are good enough. Off they went with MY Landy for a spin and were gone for hours and hours...ok they were gone less than five minutes but by the time they returned I had developed a pair of new stomach ulcers and they had very straight faces.

They got out and walked over to that little room that all MOT stations have and disappeared inside. One walked out empty handed followed quite some time later by the other who had a bit of white paper in hos hand. I liked the old MOT's because you could see the different colour and knew you had passed but these bloody new ones are white the same as the fail sheet so I stood there trying to look cool calm and unconcerned of the outcome from this hour and five minute grilling of a test they had put my project and I through when the chap burst into a big grin and told me IT HAD ONLY BLOODY PASSED!!!

The relief was overwhelming along with the beaming grin I now donned like a kid after he just got the best present ever! There were three advisories and he run me through these and even pointed out where on the Landy they were and what best to do with them which not many places take the time to do these days and it was much appreciated. So at this point I am going to say thanks to the guys at Nottingham Car Care Ltd and say to anyone who has a classic these guys are well worth a visit because they are a rare breed of folk who understand how they work.

The Advisories? Ok then they were as follows:-

1. Offside lower leaf spring bush has slight wear.
2. Evidence of offside front tyre fouling.
3. Slight fluid weep from offside swivel joint.

Nothing there too bad considering the rebuild that has been done so far and these bits can be sorted while I await a registration number.

It was a much more enjoyable drive home as I took a bit more notice of the Landy and got to know it a bit noting the bangs groans and clanks he made as he drove on. It was pointed out to me the Landy is running very lean so I need to sort that as it did feel a little underpowered even for a heavy old lump.

Soon enough we were back on the driveway and with some reluctance I switched off the engine because I know it will be at least a few weeks before I get to drive it again but now I have all of the paperwork needed for the DVLA well apart from the tax man but DVLA who I spoke to today told me to send it all in now anyway because as I have said before in an earlier post they might not check for import duty and even if they do it's with the Tax man directly so a crossover should happen in paperwork. Hell who am I to argue I will send them the forms and see what happens!
So the worst is done. I bought an old wreck and now I have my first Land Rover complete with an MOT. It is elating to look at it and think "I did that" There are a few more bits to do but those bits are now at my leisure and more in the way to personalise and make it mine. There will be more updates this is not the end and I am already considering the next project in the back of my mind but without further ado folks I would like to introduce you all to "Mator" my Land Rover.

www.justturned40.co.uk

vec150

Re: The project has landed!

1st class we'll done.

Greenie85

Re: The project has landed!

Bloody nice one mate!

Discokids

Re: The project has landed!

Jolly good! Great result.

raywin

Re: The project has landed!

Nice to see all that hard work rewarded well done!

Iann

Re: The project has landed!

Nice one fella

whens the road trip planned :)

min200

Re: The project has landed!

Quote:

Originally Posted by Iann (Post 3344796)
Nice one fella

whens the road trip planned :)

Soon as it has plates ;)

min200

Re: The project has landed!

Thanks everyone I am pretty damned chuffed :)

aaronmorris

Re: The project has landed!

Top news min.

easye1

Re: The project has landed!

very well done min.....

err, your slight weep front swivle, did you put straight oil in or one
shot grease///
as mine had more than a weep but the chrome was good so I
emptied a small grease gun load of molygrease into the hub via the
top up hole, it silenced a clattering velosity joint on lock and the
weep only notices on very hot days after driving it...
but take advice from others about my cure all..
the carb can be rechecked for float level hight, and an partially
blocked main jet, or jet size to correct specs, bearing in mind
someone may have reduced the main jet size for other reasons...
but saying that, bet it warmed up nice running lean.....
just a small point, has the ignition timing been checked for correct
advance, as i`ve known cars to show signs of being weeak on
mixture but been running with retarded ignition settings...(just
saying)/

but bloody well done that man...
ian..

min200

Re: The project has landed!

A mine of information as always Ian :) Thank you chap!

min200

Re: The project has landed!

Mail and Money

Main
Posted by min200 Sat, January 10, 2015 19:56:32

Now the initial elation of getting Mator's MOT has passed I looked into the final steps of the registration forms and total costs of the project.

I sat last night going over the DVLA forms making sure all the correct boxes were ticked that the paperwork they require was copied and in order then that the cheque had been written for the correct amount and made out to them along with the precious MOT certificate all was put into an envelope which was duly taped shut just to make sure it all stayed in there until it arrived in Swansea.

This precious cargo was then posted this morning at 8am so it would catch the Saturday post and arrive hopefully at the mercy of those registration gods that will grant me a magic number to allow me to start playing on and off road in my painstakingly rebuilt motor. Wifey has already asked what I am going to build next because "you will finish the last bits off quick then start moping around annoying me because you have nothing else to distract you"...ain't love grand eh! She is right though I will have to source something else and I have a couple of ideas in the pipeline so watch this space.

Now onto the final figures of the build. I have scratched my head and looked at a couple of receipts so I am pretty sure everything I have spent is included. The final price is what it cost not only to rebuild the Land Rover but what it cost to get it onto the road legally including insurance for the year and six months tax which are a big chunk of change.

Landy Project Costs

Land Rover £375

Sanding Discs £11.70

Ignition Barrel £20

Heritage letter £21.75

2x Batteries and rear 1/4 light £35

Pair Battery Terminal Clamps £3.99

Floor pan nuts & bolts £6.50

Grinding disc £2.25

Under Seal £8.99

Complete set of lights £85

5 Litres Primer £24.99

4 Discovery Wheels £10.20

Rear Door £21.00

Front Door £20.00

Handbrake spring £1.50

2 Discovery wheels

Two seatbelts

Wing Mirror

2 Headlight surrounds

2 headlight frames £60

2 Front Doors £60

Nato Green Paint £36

Rear Window Seal and insert £9.99

Wiring connectors £3.00

2 tins of silver metal paint £7.00

Fuses & Sandpaper £4.50

5x tins black spray £5.00

5x more tins black spray £5.00

Clutch fluid

Exhaust putty

WD40 £8.49

Car Boot Bits £13

Front & rear shocks £59.45

Front & rear brake rebuild kits £81.62

Fuel tank & filler £40

Wheels complete with tyres £250

Fuel pump

Fuel hose

Indicator stalk

Bonnet strap

Brake switch

Fuel pump gasket

Fuel line clips £67.74

24v Wiper motor

24v flasher relay

24v heater

24v front loom

oil cooler

Door tops x2

Rear bench seat £67.50

Roof rack £100

Wheel nuts £8

Brake pipe kit £39

Wheels & Tyres £250

Exhaust System & Flexi hose pipes £66

Number plate light £5

Seat set £90

Fuel tank and service parts £136

Seat belts £61

Rear seat brackets £10

Spark plugs £30

Brake switch £17

MOT £30

CREDIT FOR BITS SOLD OFF OF PROJECT £502

TOTAL REBUILD COST £1708.16

Insurance £150

6 Months Tax £126.50

DVLA Registration fee £55

TOTAL ON THE ROAD PRICE...... £2039.66

So the total "Rebuild" cost was £1708.16 and the "On the Road" price worked out as a whopping £2039.66! Now folks that is seriously not a bad price for a "rebuilt" Land Rover that is now worth a bit more than that if you wanted to buy it finished off of the shelf. OK I admit it doesn't include all of the what probably would work out at a 100 hours plus that I have put into it but as a home grown rebuild project that has kept me off of the cigs and using the cash I would have spent on those cigs instead of smoking it it really is a good price!

The bill will now increase a little as it is personalised by me but that's by the by because the aim at the start of the rebuild if you can remember that far back was to see if I could make something half decent on a tight budget and well even if I say so myself whilst blowing my own trumpet a bit I have done exactly that! I didn't start with a pile of cash in the bank or bottom drawer I used my "Pocket money" that I used to spend on cigs each month and quite often ran short of money and had to wait to buy bits. The project itself gave back in the form of military bits removed and sold on to enthusiasts that want to keep certain models "original" and good luck to them but this project was mine and I have made it unique to me in small but important to me ways.

I have heard folk say that the Land Rover prices are rising especially on Defenders and Series models and I have to admit I have seen these jump in the nine months of this build. BUT there are still bargains to be had if you are lucky to stumble across one as I did so if you want one keep looking because they are snapped up pretty damned quick!

So in short folks I have succeeded in getting a knackered old Landy rebuilt and back on the road for about two grand. This is no mean feet as I didn't have the cash when I started and I didn't know what I was doing really as I had never had a Land Rover before! If a plank like me can do it and if you are sat reading this thinking I couldn't do that just buy a book, join the forums so you can get valuable advice and jump right in.

There will be times you doubt yourself then times when you hurt yourself you will want to cry you will laugh out loudly but you will end up feeling good about yourself when you look upon that little job that you thought was beyond your remit but it sits there in front of you fixed anyway!

Upon reflection I have loved every high and low of this rebuild I have loved the comments on the forums of encouragement and the micky taking when I have assumed or written something wrong. Thanks folks for coming along on this journey with me you have kept me focused on the right road and kept me writing.

All the best
Nick.

www.justturned40.co.uk

min200

11th-January-2015 15:48

Re: The project has landed!

Quick fix.

Main

Posted by min200 Sun, January 11, 2015 15:46:19

Now the MOT is done I popped on the light protectors.

EvoQued

Re: The project has landed!

Quote:

Originally Posted by min200 (Post 3346195)
Mail and Money
www.justturned40.co.uk

I don't post on these forums that much, but this reflective post is well worth the credit =) Nicely documented & rewarding end to it all.

On to.. the next? ;)

min200

Re: The project has landed!

Thank you that is much appreciated :)

As for the next well watch this space...

easye1

Re: The project has landed!

Quote:

> Originally Posted by min200 (Post 3347221)
> *Thank you that is much appreciated :)*
>
> *As for the next well watch this space...*

a chinook is far too much of an excorsize min.....lol

but you can park the landie inside... ;)

min200

Re: The project has landed!

If im honest not sure what to go for but there a few ideas kicking about at the moment ;)

Got ot be cheap and cheerful though!

Dan_Trials   11th-January-2015 20:33

Re: The project has landed!

How I hadn't seen this thread before I do not know, but I did on
Friday night and since then I have been reading it post by post
between getting nagged at to do house related chores and getting a
sneaky bit of time in the shed on my own projects. It has been
amazing to see the transformation and how it has been written in
such an entertaining style! I felt like I was riding the emotional roller
coaster with you on the build up to and during the MOT then I
actually got goose bumps as I read the part where the tester
declared it had passed! Hope you get the rest of the paperwork tied
up and you finally get to enjoy the results of your hard work!

min200   11th-January-2015 21:05

Re: The project has landed!

Dan that is probably THE best review I have ever received so thank
you chap no really you have made me smile.

I will keep on writing my Landy related drivel on here as and when I
do a few bits and start taking Mator on new adventures.

Now for the shameless plug even though I usually stick the web
address on the end of my posts I will carry on writing about other
bits on my blog unlandy related as well as so feel free to come
along ;)

www.justturned40.co.uk

Dan_Trials

Re: The project has landed!

Quote:

Haha great I got copied and pasted on to Facephuck proper
famous now! Seriously it has been great following the build in
the 72hr crash course version I got. Your writing style goes
great with both beer and a take away and coffee and bacon
rolls! I will indeed check out your blog, keep the updates and
funny stories coming!

min200

Re: The project has landed!

Cheers fella I will try :)

What me proper famous on Facewipe! What ever next lol

marccleave

Re: The project has landed!

Loved reading through this. Excellent pictures and fantastic work on the Land-Rover! Bet you can't wait to get your registration plate and actually drive it now its MOT'd!!! :D

I know the feeling/pain with the registering a vehicle process. I'm also currently going through the process of registering a vehicle (Non Land-Rover, also only has two wheels!), V55/5 and all that. Except there was slight confusion when HMRC/National Clearance Hub sent the import forms to the Personal Transport Unit in Dover. TWICE. So two months wasted while they confirmed duty/VAT had or hadn't been paid. Got my forms off to the DVLA last week so hopefully hear a reply this week.

Keep up the great work! Spill the beans on what you're thinking on next? :) Go on... throw some ideas onto the table for discussion! ;)

min200

11th-January-2015 22:34

Re: The project has landed!

Driving it will be fun and I can't wait to offroad and have some fun!

What's next well...honestly not sure. Considering a bike or another landy based motor. Another idea doing teh rounds is building one for the charity I worked with last year and then selling/auctioning it on to raise funds for the kids BUT that will take soem sorting with A) getting the donor vehicle donated B) getting a or some sponsors onboard for parts and C) Some folk to help then finally D) Somewhere local to do it as I am running out of room on the driveway. The charity thing does appeal and I could write the blog the same way again as we go along but with a few new faces involved as well to keep it fresh?

What do you all think?

Discokids

11th-January-2015 22:59

Re: The project has landed!

Charity project sounds good, can possibly assist with C. Have tools and a bit of knowledge, and I'm not too far from you.

Dan_Trials

11th-January-2015 23:27

Re: The project has landed!

Good idea, doing what you enjoy while helping others!

min200

12th-January-2015 07:06

Re: The project has landed!

I like the idea too it will just take a bit of organising behind the scenes first ;)

Dan_Trials

12th-January-2015 22:21

Re: The project has landed!

Quote:

Originally Posted by min200 (Post 3348186)
I like the idea too it will just take a bit of organising behind the scenes first ;)

Well best of luck with it, and of course... we need a build thread! :p :D

min200

Re: The project has landed!

Oh there would be a thread ;)

Dan_Trials

Re: The project has landed!

Quote:

> Originally Posted by min200 (Post 3349622)
> *Oh there would be a thread ;)*

Good lad ;) :D

min200

Re: The project has landed!

Forms and Frustration

Land Rover Rebuild
Posted by min200 Wed, January 14, 2015 20:32:22

When I say "Forms and Frustration" as the title of this entry (there's a good word it always makes me think of the old paper diaries we all said we didn't write as kids) it's really me just being an impatient bugger.

I see the weather forecasters are predicting doom and gloom with high winds more snow than on the set of game of thrones and then the inevitable flooding when it all melts away again and what would the ideal motor for this be I hear you ask? Well a newly rebuilt Land Rover should do the job nicely I would think!

Listen to me moaning I do apologise folks it's not like I would even take it out if the registration turned up in the morning there are a couple of bits I want to sort first including changing over the gearbox mounts as they are past there best and after all this time and effort I have put into the old boy a little more wont hurt. The steering wheel needs to be set straight instead of 90 degrees out as it will drive me insane each time I touch it! Oh I need to sort out a 24v to 12v dropper for the CB and there is a Land Rover badge on the way too...bloody hell it's turning into a shopping list on here now!

So each evening when I return from work and look with hope at my coffee table where the post gets dumped I feel a little disappointed there's no registration for me but I know it's too soon the DVLA have probably only just opened the letter from me if I am lucky so expecting to see what wont be there is daft...or maybe it's just a little bit of hope.

min200   15th-January-2015 20:18

Re: The project has landed!

NO GO ON REGISTRATION

Land Rover Rebuild
Posted by min200 Thu, January 15, 2015 20:17:13

Bugger. Just bugger. I arrived home this evening to find two brown envelopes waiting for me one form the tax man and one from the DVLA so I got a little excited that was until I opened them...

The tax man wants more information and will I call them about the application for a NOVA number which I will do in the morning. Well that could swing either way I guess form good to bad but the letter form the DVLA is the real problem.

The DVLA want me to send them either MOD papers MOD654 / MOD654B or a Certificate of Origin from the MOD. I don't have any of these forms as I explained when I first called them before I started out on this project and was told not to worry! Well now I am getting worried...

I have had a dig around the tinterweb and can find no information on how I could obtain this sort of paperwork 17 years after the vehicle has been released from the MOD so if any of you good folk have experienced this and know the way forward it would be much appreciated. Everywhere is closed now so I cant talk directly to anyone until the morning so I suppose it will be a long night...

www.justturned40.co.uk

Discokids

Re: The project has landed!

In my experience, ring them and discuss. If they sound confused and can't instantly help you without saying something like 'err' or 'oohh' or 'can I just ask a colleague', then they're wasting your time, and possibly making it worse. hang up and call back and eventually you will get somebody who understands your situation.

marccleave   15th-January-2015 21:43

Re: The project has landed!

With regards to the tax man and NOVA number... I had no end of fun with that. Had to fill in a C&E109, provide a covering letter, etc and send it to the National Clearance Hub. Who ended up screwing up and sending it to the Personal Transport Unit in Dover. After much faffing turns out the importer hadn't paid VAT & IMPORT DUTY so I ended up paying that. But you won't have any due on this as its not an import. After that went through got the NOVA number and could carry on with the DVLA registration.

I originally sent the V55 in late November then the C&E109 in early December. I have only just recently received the V5C for the vehcle. So that kinda shows how long it could take. Once I got the NOVA number it took the DVLA ~5 working days to give me the V5C / registration for the vehicle so DVLA isn't the worrying part. Its HMRC and The National Clearance Hub which royally screwed me over.

Been pulling my hair out for the past several weeks but its so worth it when you finally get the registration back from the DVLA.

Chin up and GOOD LUCK. I wouldn't wish doing this registration process on anybody.

SpiritMR   16th-January-2015 01:55

Re: The project has landed!

Just read this from start to finish.

Absolutely awesome read. Really makes me want to get one to.replace to dinged Disco.

min200

Re: The project has landed!

Quote:

> Originally Posted by SpiritMR (Post 3353696)
> *Just read this from start to finish.*
>
> *Absolutely awesome read. Really makes me want to get one to.replace to dinged Disco.*

Thanks :) It is worth it even with the current registration issues!

Thanks to you good folk that have replied about the current problems the Tax man and DVLA open in a few minutes so the calls will start then...ready get set.....

min200

Re: The project has landed!

Dentists and Dial Tones

Land Rover Rebuild
Posted by min200 Fri, January 16, 2015 19:06:12

Well the day started off with a visit to the Dentists. I don't like
Dentists I know they have a hard job staring into peoples sometimes
stinky mouths all day but I am pretty sure mine is a bit of a sadist
who enjoys inflicting pain in fact I am pretty sure the only reason he
wears a mask is so you cannot see him smiling.

He told me that "This might have a hot spot here and there" as it felt
like he was cutting my gums off with a blunt knife...you have gotta
love having a deep clean. I am not a small man and most of the time
I face the worlds problems head on not fearlessly but with a
determination to get through and past them but stick me in a
Dentists chair and I am five year old who just wants his Mummy!
Still that was soon over and the next problem of the day had to be
sorted.

First stop was the DVLA call about the rejected application for my
Land Rover...Well all I am going to say at this point is always put a
covering letter in with your application it just may save you some
time worry and heartache. I have returned some forms to them and
I will write up exactly what next week because I am doubtful that it
is all they will want so watch this space.

Then it was the turn of the Tax Man this was not a call I was looking
forward to either because they wanted me to contact them about the
monies owing on the Land Rover. How a Landy from the MOD could
owe Import Duty and VAT was beyond me so I picked up the phone
and with my stomach turning butterflies I dialled them.

I would like to point out at this point I had spent most of the night tossing and turning had taken a visit to the dentist for some torture and just dealt with the DVLA my God I didn't want to make a call that would cost me more cash I didn't have for a car that I cannot drive but hell it just had to be done. So with a deep breath I gave the reference number and waited for my pants to be pulled down.

Ever had one of those experiences that when they are over you blink to yourself in pleasant surprise and the day just feels a little better? Well I had that today with of all people the Tax Man. Turns out that they had entered the landy in as a brand new vehicle and had since realised their mistake and rectified it and another letter is in the post explaining this. They also apologised...yes that's right the Tax Man said sorry for the cock up and I hope it hasn't caused you too much worry! So fingers crossed as that bit is now done and dusted that the next DVLA instalment isn't too painful either.
With all of that over I went out to potter around on Mator as there were a few little bits wanting doing. I started by fitting his new spare wheel cover.

I am pretty sure they have sent the wrong size out as it seems a couple of inches too small so looks a bit rubbish really. It can stay on for now though to help keep the winter off of the padlock keeping the wheel in place.
At the MOT I noticed the spring on the drivers side window wiper arm wasn't that good so I treated myself to a pair of new wiper arms.
At least I should now be able to see out of a bit of the window in the rain! I then fired up the old boy so he could warm through a touch and to just hear the engine run while I tackled the steering wheel. It sat at the vertical instead of the horizontal to and from the MOT annoying the hell out of me so I popped off the center cap undid the nut and turned it around to sit the right way up.
By now the engine had warmed up nicely so I thought I might have a bash at improving the carb mixture as it was running very lean on the MOT test and did feel a little underpowered while driving it. After

asking some cleverer folk than me on the forums I was informed where the mixture screw was.

As I turned it I could hear the engine pick up and it was nice to lose the "popping" noise when I took my foot off of the accelerator.

Then with a smug feeling of accomplishment and the tension of the last 24 hours easing away I set to fitting the window locks onto the doors. This didn't take long which was good because I was starting to loose the feeling in my fingers to the cold.

This was enough for the day I was getting really cold and tired and I decided that cooking dinner was a good option seeing as Wifey has a bloody awful cold and her coughing and sneezing over the food didn't seem like a particularly appetizing situation.

www.justturned40.co.uk

min200

17th-January-2015 16:45

Re: The project has landed!

Badges & Spares

Land Rover Rebuild
Posted by min200 Sat, January 17, 2015 16:40:54

You have got to love a long weekend off. Turn away now if you wish because I would just like to point out I am into day two of a four day weekend and boy do I need it! Nothing like some down time to kick back and relax... Yea right like I would ever just kick back and relax but I am enjoying just pottering around doing as I please more or less.

After a lazy start with tea in bed then a big fat sausage cob Wifey and I pottered along a riverside before getting home and me deciding that now would be a good time to sort out the sheds and greenhouse seeing as I am getting to saturation point of junk spares and clutter that most of I don't really need.

All I managed was the greenhouse and shed one before the light gave out but I am now the proud owner of one pile of junk to go to the dump and another pile to Ebay off so three guesses what I will be doing this evening!

The best part of the day though was when my youngest daughter decided to tell me that a good friend had dropped me off an old Land Rover badge for Mator five hours after he had done so and three hours after I had got in. Bloody teenagers when I asked where it was she just looked at me like I was stupid and said "On the dining room table" as if this was the most obvious place for something to be left as well as the first and only place I would look when arriving home "just in case" something had arrived. Still I am pleased as punch with it and it looks like the old motor is properly dressed now it is on. Still a couple of bits I would like to fit in around everything else this weekend but whether I get the chance will be another thing....

min200

Re: The project has landed!

Droppers and Damp

Land Rover Rebuild
Posted by min200 Mon, January 19, 2015 16:12:33

Well I made right royal arse out of myself and it was online where everybody can now see for ever or until the human race dies out whichever comes first.

Now you see I was clearing out my sheds and I cam e across an old 24v-12v dropper I forgot I had bought as part of a job lot and this is a good turn of events as I needed to buy one for my new CB that

Wifey bought me for Christmas. I took a quick look at it and its three wires and wondered to myself what wire did what so a quick photo on my mobile and it was uploaded online with exactly that question.

But being a busy chap I failed to see what was right in front of my face that being the printed instructions on the sticker that is on the dropper that everyone and hos mate saw before me and quite rightly then proceeded to take the micheal out of my utter stupidity. I started to blame my eyesight but in writing the sentence started I laughing at myself and realised I wouldn't buy that so why would anyone else? Sometimes you just have to admit you are a tool it is just far easier than digging yourself a grave!

Now then seeing as that embarrassment is done with I had a day off all to myself today and decided to change over the gearbox mounts because in all fairness the old ones were looking a little bit ropey at best. Shouldn't take long that eh? What an hour max just support the gearbox whip the old ones off one side at a time and drop in the new ones.

Yea right why do I still think these things you would have thought I would have learnt better by now.

The nearside first and as you can see once I jacked it up a touch the mount broke up so it really needed doing. Could I get a socket or a spanner in anywhere near the rubber mount nuts either end no no I could not so no worries I thought I will just drop off the whole bracket instead. The bottom one came off fine but the bracket attached to the gearbox fought me for nearly two hours with seized nuts locking nut flaps in unreachable spots and the exhaust thought it would be just a bot funny to be in the way as much as possible especially at the angle where I needed to put a spanner.

I muttered and groaned swore under my breath and fought on...it fought back at every turn the fact it was freezing cold really helped out each time I slipped and banged a hand against metal but I won in the end. The rubber mount was now in two bits still attached to each bracket but I was done with being nice so out came my favourite bosh it tool the grinder. Within two minutes the brackets were clear and even though it was a bit of a pig to put back on it went on easily enough compared to getting it off.

Now at this point I was thinking to myself that I was bloody cold and maybe the offside mount would be ok really and wouldn't need doing...obviously it did so with gusto I had to muster from the depths I set to getting the old one off. It came off easily on all bolts too easily I mean its an old Land Rover there was going to have to be a price because there always is...

I looked around and was happy to find the new mount sat there with new bolts just wanting to be fitted. Nothing bad seemed to be lurking about I could even account for all of my tools so I set to apprehensively putting it back together...then the snow started.
I kid you not whatever forces are at work in this world do like having a laugh with me I must be like their personal play thing and not in a good way! I lay there underneath the Landy wondering why my legs were starting to feel really cold then I looked outwards and started to chuckle to myself because there was nothing to be doe at this point at the blizzard that descended in a matter of minutes. Still the mount had to be fitted as I didn't want to leave the gearbox balancing on a jack all night so I spent ten more minutes with my legs sticking out from underneath the motor slowly turning white. Mounts done and me feeling happy it was all over I threw my tools in my shed noted to myself the damned white stuff really was settling and went on for some lunch. I came out an hour later after warming through to post some parcels and all of the snow had gone but after a cold morning lying on concrete I decided enough is enough for one day and I will tackle the electrical issue I have at the weekend.

easye1   19th-January-2015 19:18

Re: The project has landed!

great write ups as usual min...
listen, your comments on lying on cold concrete -
in my shed I have a boot lining from a mondeo ghia that went to the
breakers, plus a rather large and thick cardboard box thats folded
flat...lol..NO - your not having it, but for my old bones it helps in
laying on cold concrete...
you really must source some sort of barrier from cold concrete, and a
supply of cardboard is so good for catching dripped oils while
servicing & topping up, then chuck the smelly cardboard away...EP90
is evil stuff that you dont want to lay in..
Me being with old bones, I also nave an old leather chairs cushion
that does stirling work in sitting on or laying my head on while under
landies also....

good hunting, and thanks for great reading again..

min200   19th-January-2015 19:28

Re: The project has landed!

I do have a bit of old lino I use but a warm mattress would suffice
lol.

Thanks for the compliment again chap I do like to drone on!

taylorslandy72

Re: The project has landed!

Looks great, rub down Saturday, hand painted by Sunday! Nice and original, good buy there

min200

24th-January-2015 19:11

Re: The project has landed!

Broken Babygrows & Blown Switches

Land Rover Rebuild
Posted by min200 Sat, January 24, 2015 19:09:20

No news on the registration but hopefully that's good in itself but the brake lights have been playing up again. They were sticking on then turning off then not working at all but after being parked up so long I have been lucky the rest of the electrics are playing nice.

I checked connections all the way through the lines they were fine as well as the power from front to back so I thought it must be the relay then seeing as it looks a little rusty. I just happened to have one in a box at the back of the shed amongst a box full of 24v spares I got months ago so I took the light box apart and found that just popping the relay out was not going to be that straight forward...of course not it is my old landy.

See there was a relay at the back the one that could not possibly be more awkward to get to to remove if it had two bolts on the inside among the wiring to remove to get it out...oh yea it did have two bolts on the inside among the wiring to get it off and I had to twist and bend to get my fat fingers in place then just as I was contorting in a position worthy of the karma sutra there was a rip as the backside of my babygrow gave out under the strain of my ass trying to escape from it.

With a jump on my part at the noise the sudden cold and worry it was the seat I had broken my hand slipped and I jammed my fingers down onto the back of the six way switch stabbed myself in the hand with a screwdriver then sat down with a bump so as not to frighten any passing pedestrians.

By now I was getting a bit peeved but I nearly had the bugger out, the relay not my ass, and it was soon swapped over with the replacement. This made no difference at all to the performance of the brake lights so I got out a replacement switch and popped it in place on the back of the servo. Now they worked again just fine but this is how the other two were and they didn't last long but upon advice from those who know better than me on such electrical matters I have ordered a decent make replacement switch ready for when this one burns out along with a new babygrow before I ruin all of my clothes again.

Re: The project has landed!

And it is complete.

Land Rover Rebuild
Posted by min200 Thu, January 29, 2015 20:41:18

The paperwork for Mator's first registration has been back with the DVLA for the second time for two weeks now. I have been stressing worrying driving myself around in circles tying myself up in knots creating scenarios that it would be sent back to me rejected again even though I have done everything the DVLA has asked.
I suppose I should explain what they did ask for after the first rejection. I was dumbfounded when it was returned rejected as I had sent everything that was requested but now the person dealing with my request had decided that I needed to send in the original MOD paperwork from when it was demobbed as well.
17 years have since passed since its demob so that paperwork doesn't exist any more so I called in a state of anxious worry the next morning to be told by the same team that this was not needed seeing as it had been sat around in a field for that time so could I send it all back with a covering letter and "whatever else you have for it".
I explained I had the MERLIN report showing all relevant MOD details and they were over the moon about that so I dully sent it all off the very next morning.

Well today the insurance company that gave me 60 days to get the registration sent a snotty email wanting it within 14 days so my worrying mind couldn't take the suspense any more so I called DVLA direct again today to see what was happening because the cheque we sent in to pay for the tax etc still had not been cashed. After being asked a minefield of questions determining the time and consistency of my last poo the lovely lady told me that yes it has all been approved and your Land Rover now has a registration number.

I was over the moon and even better she gave me the Registration over the phone because they are now allowed to do that so I could tell the insurance company. I felt like a weight had been lifted off of my shoulders and my Land Rover is now mine because I can drive it around for at least five miles before it breaks down but I don't care because I will just fix it and do it all again!
When I arrived home even more good news in that the V5 was sat there on the coffee table as well so I can go straight out on Saturday morning and get the number plates made up!

This really is the point where it all feels complete that the months of hard work sorting out the MOT and then the worrying myself daft for a fortnight over something I could not control was really worth it. Don't get me wrong I don't recommend being a worrying pillock like me because it is pointless and I know that but it does not stop me from doing it though over the stupid things but the opposite side of it is the high you get when it all comes together.

Man it feels so good to have built something like this and of course a logbook that states my Landy has had no previous keepers ;)

Discokids

Re: The project has landed!

Well done Min! Got there in the end. Why wait til Saturday? Snow will have melted by then!

min200

Re: The project has landed!

LOL First time I will get a chance with work chap...unfortunately

Jam1

Re: The project has landed!

Congrats :) enjoy it.

min200

Re: The project has landed!

Oh I am planning to :) Thanks ;)

min200

Re: The project has landed!

Number Plates & Cleaning

Land Rover Rebuild
Posted by min200 Sat, January 31, 2015 16:18:32

I awoke to the sight if snow falling yet again and it was pretty bloody cold to boot. The cough that my eldest daughter had donated to me overnight had settled in for the long haul and my bones ache from a mixture of hard work with germs...the day ahead didn't bode well. The plan was get some plates made up and go and have a bit of a play in the Landy but seeing as I was moving at the pace of an elderly snail plans were thrown out of the window.

I have worked so hard then worried so much on this old motor that another day wont hurt. The number plates were bought when I finally ventured out then as I went to fit them I saw that the wiring was out and about from tracing the brake light issue last weekend so I set to putting all of that back into place. That done it was time to fit the plates! I carefully marked them up in a geeky way as to where the holes needed to be gently drilled through and after laughing at the guys in the shops who wanted £2:79 for a pair of capped number plate screws I bolted them on instead.
I mean what difference does it make when it comes to me breaking them off road in a few weeks?? because I will I am sure and in anticipation of this I have just ordered a cheap replacement off of fleabay to carry around in the back.

The tools from the rebuild that have lived in the back of it for months have been taking out and put away properly for the first time in forever the boot now seems very bare.

Still feeling rough I have decided to wait until tomorrow to take a proper test drive out along with the fact that seeing as I worry like a woman as you all know the RAC membership I have bought doesn't kick in the recovery side until tomorrow afternoon I shall err upon the side of caution to start with.
Next steps will be the rear interior the winterised lining is coming off and will need to be replaced but that will be over time along with having to wait for warmer weather to paint the inside.
But guess what folks? I am only going out driving in it on the road for real tomorrow and I cannot wait :) Now where did my Lemsip go???

elan23

Re: The project has landed!

Hearty congrats, typical of the lurgy to strike now. Makes me want to start on mine, oh... good luck on the bidding for the coil !!

min200

Re: The project has landed!

Quote:

Originally Posted by elan23 (Post 3374628)
oh... good luck on the bidding for the coil !!

Thats yours then is it! lol Now I know I would like a discount please ;)

min200

Re: The project has landed!

You couldn't make it up...

Land Rover Rebuild
Posted by min200 Sun, February 01, 2015 12:27:01

Well the sun was shining I only had a couple of chores to do and Wifey was off out so today was the day Mator and I were going on our first proper drive. I had planned to take lots of pictures of it in different places just to show it out and about but first I had a couple of things to do.

Soon enough the bike was fuelled up the parcels dropped of for delivery from some junk I had sold on Ebay and I was sitting in my Landy feeling good with a grin onmy face ready to roll.

I popped the keys in the ignition turned them to get only a flat battery click. I mean for Gods sake I only had it running yesterday but then a memory popped in of me thinking the lights looked a little on teh dim side but I put it down to the sun being out for a change.

So I dragged the batteries out and put them on charge then set to seeing if it was anything obvious as to why the batteries weren't charging. First and final stop was at the generator where it was obvious that the main cable that comes out of it to the shunt box was very loose. That'll probably be it then because any more loose and it would have dropped off.

Next chance to drive the old boy??? That will be next weekend then...bugger.

Dev

Re: The project has landed!

Great thread. Could you put black number plates back on or do you have to fit white and yellow plates?

min200
1st-February-2015 14:47

Re: The project has landed!

Has to be White and Yellow due to it's age...shame though black would have looked the muts!

Dev
1st-February-2015 16:47

Re: The project has landed!

It would, it's absolutely begging for black plates.

min200
6th-February-2015 20:59

Re: The project has landed!

Charging and Connections

Land Rover Rebuild
Posted by min200 Fri, February 06, 2015 20:54:57

Mator has decided that even though he has been loved and lavished attention on over the last ten months he did not want to play out. He was not going to give up any electrical power had gone into a full scale sulk not even pointing me in the right direction of where to look to start.

So I asked those good folk online in various forums and got a dozen different maybes so I started with the Alternator. I stripped it out of the engine and suck it indoors because what I was about to do was fiddly as hell for my monkey fingers and sitting down at the dining table to do it seemed to be a good idea. What I forgot was that I was not the only one off of work today and just when I could not be making more of a mess Wifey walked in the door with a look of horror on her face at the various bits of very greasy alternator gubbings strewn across the tabletop. I don't think I deserved the tirade of abuse that followed seeing as I had put newspaper down on the table before I started but it seems that this was not quite enough to appease the woman of my life so I suppose that will cost me a bunch of flowers tomorrow.

Anyway I stripped the back of the alternator off to check and clean the connections and bushes.
It was filthy in there and greasy as hell so a good clean out with Meths sorted that problem and the bushes were showing wear but still had some life left in them so I put it all back together did not loose any of the tiny screws and refitted into engine bay. The key turned the engine fired up so I checked the batteries they were still only showing 24v.

Bugger.

I resigned myself to the cost of a new alternator but I asked again on the forums and was told to run through it all again checking for loose connections etc. One comment stood out as the chap said "check the cables going into the regulator box are not over tightened and popped the retaining D ring out as this will cause the wiring to work loose" Now this struck a cord because way back when I had started to strip the landy down for rebuild I undid a lot of that cabling by mistake but hell it could not be that easy could it?

Yes it could. In my early day eagerness I had over tightened them and popped out the D ring so I put it all back together reconnected the batteries and fired up the engine...
A healthy 28+volts coming through and charging nicely. So a days worth of buggering about because I buggered up one connection months and months ago.

Still at least it kept me away from Wifeys wrath for a few hours.

www.justturned40.co.uk

Land Raver

6th-February-2015 22:31

Re: The project has landed!

Enjoyed reading this. Well done with the refurb. Looking forward to seeing some pictures of it being used in anger :)

min200

6th-February-2015 23:01

Re: The project has landed!

Quote:

Originally Posted by Land Raver (Post 3381764)
Enjoyed reading this. Well done with the refurb. Looking forward to seeing some pictures of it being used in anger :)

Thanks I hope I made you smile at some point! It will be used now I know I wont get stuck out with a flat battery...It will be something else that breaks now instead ;)

min200

8th-February-2015 09:31

Re: The project has landed!

The First Time

Land Rover Rebuild
Posted by min200 Sun, February 08, 2015 09:30:19

Well I sit here working up the bravery to take Mator out for his first run. We wont be going far just around the city to do a few chores but I feel as nervous as a virgin on prom night.

This is all depending on whether I get to the petrol station before he runs out as he is running on fumes!

See you all on the other side...

woody13

8th-February-2015 11:46

Re: The project has landed!

Looks like a good base for a long term project.Gonna be looking for something like that for myself sometime soon.

Re: The project has landed!

Then there was rough running.

Land Rover Rebuild
Posted by min200 Sun, February 08, 2015 15:17:57

I apprehensively jumped into the Landy with Wifey joining me on teh passenger side and fired him up. He started well enough of course but he always has I checked the road and set off clunking through the gears wiping the condensation that appeared instantly on the windscreen all the while trying to keep his drifting steering in a semi straight line.

1/4 mile down and he is going ok as we attack the first roundabout double back and made it no worries to the petrol station.
I had noticed there was a bit of a delay when you put your foot down on the accelerator and the engine actually doing anything but I thought that might just be me some how.

We then drove a few miles to the next stop which was a sunny supermarket car park as Wifey had things to pick up but it was nice to see him in a different place for a change...

As we wandered around the Supermarket I was deep in thought as to why this delay was happening on acceleration as it seemed to be getting worse. I knew there would be teething problems but at least one trip out without one would be nice but another realisation was dawning upon me and it was one I did not really care for...I hadn't enjoyed driving him at all. I have driven plenty of them over the years so the ride handling and noise were not unexpected but I hadn't smiled once and I am hoping that it's because it's running a little rough and once I have fixed that I will enjoy him again.

Maybe I just enjoyed the rebuild...I do quite fancy doing a Discovery as in conversion to off road beast but that will be some time down the line.

Anyway after buying what looked like stuff that could have waited until the shopping was delivered tomorrow night we walked back out into the car park and I couldn't see the old boy to start with must of been the camouflage colouring and the other folk parking up with nothing better to do on a Sunday morning ;)

Driving home the flat hesitation seemed to get worse so I set to looking into it as soon as he was back onto the driveway. I checked for air intake issues but all was fine then checked the ignition system but all was good there as well but after doing some research and asking lots of questions it would seem it is the carb that is at fault which is no surprise seeing as it was parked up for years so a new one will be ordered today ready for fitting asap. I will pick up a rebuild kit as well and have a stab at rebuilding the old one as well for a new experience.

So watch this space and see if we can get the old chap running sweetly once again.

min200

8th-February-2015 18:31

Re: The project has landed!

Number plates

Land Rover Rebuild
Posted by min200 Sun, February 08, 2015 18:24:57

After fitting the rear number plate last week it became apparent that the ladder does indeed block a lot of it off but just in case plod takes a dim view of this I ordered a set of extra plates to see what I could do about it.

I thought where could I put this that it wont look stupid but it seems that this was a bit of a tall order. In the end I settled with attaching it onto the roof rack.
Looks a bit pants if I am honest but at least plod wont be on my back for something stupid.

Huddy84

8th-February-2015 21:43

Re: The project has landed!

Keep your spirits up, you can't properly adjust/fettle things till you start running about. Looks fantastic!

min200

9th-February-2015 07:17

Re: The project has landed!

Quote:

Originally Posted by Huddy84 (Post 3384355)
Keep your spirits up, you can't properly adjust/fettle things till you start running about. Looks fantastic!

Yea I know I will have a couple of rough months of teething problems but wouldn't it be nice to just jump in and drive...never in a Land Rover lol

Oh and thanks if one thing it does well is it looks good even if I say so myself :)

Afterword

So there it is my first ever stab at writing on a regular basis and I have loved it. To top it all off I have a nice Land Rover to boot that does about 10 miles to the gallon drives like the 1950's engineering it was designed from and why babies prams had leaf spring suspension fitted I have no idea because there is no ride comfort in it at all! But it had been fun so much fun in fact I cannot bring myself to ruin it off road soI have bought an old Discovery to do that in and "Brians" transformation is just beginning so why not have a nose at it on my website along with lots more in depth pictures form "Mators" rebuild.

Just pop over to www.nickysmith.me or if you want to say hello or give any feedback please feel free to drop me a line at nick@nickysmith.me

Now for the thanks...Thanks to all of the forums that had my drivel onboard www.landyzone.co.uk www.landrovers-owners-club.com and www.hmvf.co.uk
I have said thank you to Wifey at the start but I will say it again Thanks for pushing me love you are as ever right of course ;)

There are a couple of other scribbles in the making as we speak so please stay tuned for those and thank you dear reader for following from the start :)

All the best
Nick

Printed in Great Britain
by Amazon